Fossil Plants

Paul Kenrick and Paul Davis

Smithsonian Books, Washington
in association with the Natural History Museum, London

Published in the United States of America
by Smithsonian Books
in association with the Natural History Museum, London
Cromwell Road
London SW7 5BD
United Kingdom

Library of Congress Cataloging-in-Publication Data
Kenrick, Paul.
    Fossil plants / Paul Kenrick and Paul Davis.
        p.   cm.
    Includes bibliographical references and index.
    ISBN 1-58834-181-X (alk. paper)—ISBN 1-58834-156-9 (pbk. : alk. paper)
        1. Plants, Fossil. I. Davis, Paul, 1969 – II. Natural History Museum
    (London, England). III. Title.
    QE905.K46   2004
    561—dc21   2003045658

Manufactured in UK, not at government expense
11 10 09 08 07 06 05 04   5 4 3 2 1

Edited by Rebecca Harman
Designed by Mercer Design

Front cover main image: Early relative of the sumacs and poison ivy. Leaf of *Rhus stellariaefolia* (Late Eocene, Florissant, Colorado, USA).

Contents

· · · · · · · · · · · ·

Preface

Most of us experience the pleasure of cultivating plants, whether it is through the attention that we lavish upon our gardens or in the more modest aspirations embodied in the window box or the potted houseplant. Humans are uniquely sensitive to the aesthetic and culinary properties of plants, but few of us actually know much about them as living organisms. Fewer still have a sense of the long history of plant life and the wealth of information that can be unearthed from the rocks beneath our feet. This geological history is in fact surprisingly well understood, though it is mostly published in the technical literature or in specialist books. Our aim is to provide an accessible introduction to the fossil record of plants and the part that it plays in unravelling the history of life on earth.

Contemporary palaeobotanists approach their subject from two main directions, which reflect the principal areas of science in which fossil plants are of greatest relevance. Life scientists are usually motivated by a fascination for the organisms themselves. Their interests stem from the unique historical dimension that fossils bring to the study of plant evolution. Earth scientists, on the other hand, are drawn to fossil plants for what they can say about the history of our environment. Here the concern is about how one might apply information gleaned from fossils to correlate rocks across different areas and to interpret environments and climates of the past. The structure of this book reflects in part this division between the broadly geological and the broadly biological.

The fossil record is vast, and an introductory book of this nature inevitably leaves much unsaid. That which has been left out vastly outweighs that which we have been able to include, both in terms of content and detail. Our choice of topics has been dictated by several concerns. We endeavour to show something of the breadth of our knowledge of the great march of plant life through time. Where possible we have tried to illustrate the range of fossil evidence available for study. We have picked out for special treatment some areas where the study of fossil plants intersects with and informs other areas of science. We have also tried to include topics or areas that in our experience crop up regularly in the context of queries from the specialist and the non-specialist. Some of this is presented in a thematic way, and some is more suited to a narrative approach. We hope to whet the appetite of our readers, and we encourage them to pursue these subjects further in the literature cited in the reading list. Fossil plants are frequently attractive objects in their own right. They are sought out and treasured by collectors. In lifting up the rocks to peer beneath into the mysterious and ancient world of plants, we hope to illustrate something of the breadth of form and the rare beauty of plants turned to stone.

Acknowledgements

We extend special thanks to Cedric H Shute for his patience and expertise in guiding another two novices through the fossil plant collections at the Natural History Museum, London. Thanks also to David J Cantrill, Paul M Barrett, Jerry J Hooker, and Andrew J Ross for the feedback that they gave on parts of the manuscript. We thank our many colleagues who have lent us images or provided additional information, especially Chris J Cleal, Peter R Crane, Dianne Edwards, Else-Marie Friis, Jane E Francis, Patricia G Gensel, Li Cheng-Sen, Gar W Rothwell, Stephen E Scheckler, Andrew C Scott, Robert A Spicer, Paul D Taylor, Johannes C Vogel, Charles H Wellman, and Zhou Zhonghe. Many of the images are photographs taken by Philip Crabb, to whom we owe a special debt of gratitude.

Chapter One

IN THE BEGINNING
. . . .

GREEK MYTHOLOGY is rife with monstrous creatures, but few were as formidable as the *Chimaera*. This was a composite beast with the head of a lion, the body of a goat and a serpent's tail. The *Chimaera* was notorious for its ability to breath fire, but a taste for despoiling countries eventually led to its downfall. The word 'chimera' has passed into the English language meaning, in science, an organism with at least two genetically different tissues, arising either through mutation or from other sources, such as the grafting on or inserting of parts from different species. Chimeras can form naturally, and there is a growing body of evidence that points to the importance of this process long ago during the early evolution of plant and animal cells.

Plants are eukaryotes, that is each cell contains a membrane-bound nucleus. Most eukaryotes also possess several other subcellular packages or organelles, including the mitochondrion and one or more types of plastid (e.g. chloroplasts), which have specific biochemical functions. There is much scientific evidence to support the theory that organelles evolved from bacteria in a process that may well have begun as a symbiotic alliance and ended as permanent entrapment. Chloroplasts – the seat of photosynthesis – have a particularly exotic and promiscuous history involving their independent acquisition by several algal groups.

left: Pin-sized plants: the earliest land plants were very small as seen in the minute bifurcating stems terminating in expanded spore sacs of *Cooksonia pertoni*, approximately 10 mm in length (Early Devonian, Herefordshire, England).

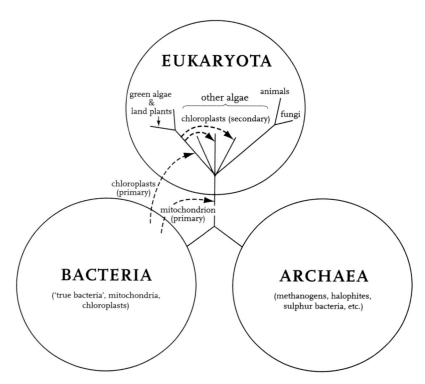

above: The three domains of life and an outline of the history of the acquisition of some of the key components of plant cells. Plants are defined here as the group comprising green algae and land plants. Chloroplasts and mitochondria derive from bacteria.

The plant cell is therefore a natural chimera, and acquired its organelles from a variety of sources. This theory underlines an additional observation that has emerged recently from the comparative study of plant genes. Algae are a very heterogeneous group of organisms, some of which may be more closely related to animals and fungi than they are to plants. The evidence from molecular biology confirms what has long been suspected, that land dwelling plants are most closely related to the green algae. Many botanists therefore group green algae and land plants together as plants, to the exclusion of all other organisms. The focus of this book is land dwelling plants, but we will begin by considering the fossil evidence for the origin of green algae and the emergence of a terrestrial flora from aquatic ancestors.

Microbes are the fundamental building blocks of plant and animal cells, and vital aspects of the machinery of eukaryotic cells were derived via multiple routes from bacterial progenitors. The study of the origin of plant life must therefore take account of the fact that plants have multiple close relatives among prokaryotes and perhaps also among other eukaryotes. Other consequences are that much of the early evolution of plants took place at the microscopic and biochemical levels, and the earliest plants were themselves unicellular organisms. This means that direct fossil evidence of the origins of plants is likely to be scant. Soft tissues, subcellular structures and biochemical pathways are rarely preserved. One further implication is that subcellular organelles such as the chloroplast had earlier histories as individuals in their own rights.

EARLY LIFE

The search for life in the earliest rocks has been likened to a forensic investigation based on a nearly empty crime scene containing a few heavily smudged fingerprints with a very real risk of cross contamination. The oldest rocks come from the Archean, which stretches from at least 4 billion to 2.5 billion years ago. The fossil record of the Archean is so sparse and scattered that this period of geological time has been compared to a medieval map, in which large blank areas are marked '*Terra incognita*'. Rocks of this age are rare because they have been subjected to 2.5 billion years of erosion, burial and subduction. Many are poorly preserved because the probability of deformation through metamorphism increases with age. Even the most pristine Archean rocks have complex histories, so exceptional care must be taken to evaluate microfossil evidence for later contamination. Despite the dearth of data and the uncertainties, there is a growing body of evidence for early life, some of which is related to plants.

The earliest evidence of cyanobacteria – the closest relatives of the plant chloroplast – comes indirectly from chemical and physical fingerprints. These need to be interpreted carefully to rule out contamination from younger sources or alteration through geological processes. Analyses are frequently

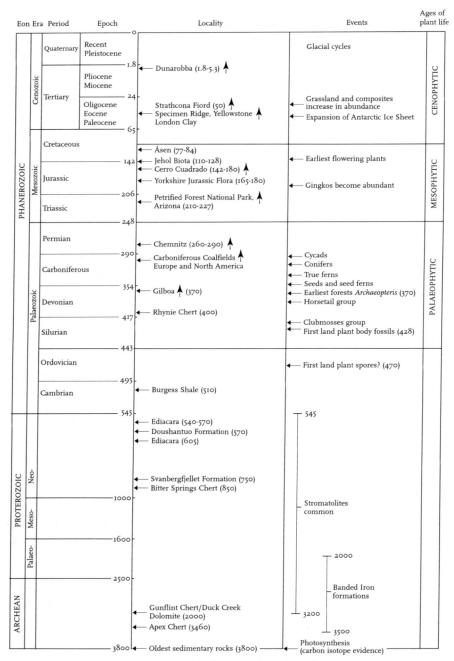

Eon	Era	Period	Epoch	Locality	Events	Ages of plant life
PHANEROZOIC	Cenozoic	Quaternary	Recent, Pleistocene	0 — Glacial cycles		CENOPHYTIC
				1.8 — Dunarobba (1.8-5.3)		
		Tertiary	Pliocene, Miocene			
			Oligocene, Eocene, Paleocene	24 — Strathcona Fiord (50), Specimen Ridge, Yellowstone, London Clay	Grassland and composites increase in abundance, Expansion of Antarctic Ice Sheet	
	Mesozoic	Cretaceous		65		MESOPHYTIC
				Åsen (77-84)		
				142 — Jehol Biota (110-128), Cerro Cuadrado (142-180)	Earliest flowering plants	
		Jurassic		Yorkshire Jurassic Flora (165-180)	Gingkos become abundant	
				206 — Petrified Forest National Park, Arizona (210-227)		
		Triassic		248		
	Palaeozoic	Permian		Chemnitz (260-290)		PALAEOPHYTIC
				290 — Carboniferous Coalfields Europe and North America	Cycads, Conifers	
		Carboniferous			True ferns, Seeds and seed ferns	
				354 — Gilboa (370)	Earliest forests Archaeopteris (370), Horsetail group	
		Devonian		Rhynie Chert (400)		
				417		
		Silurian			Clubmosses group, First land plant body fossils (428)	
				443		
		Ordovician			First land plant spores? (470)	
				495		
		Cambrian		Burgess Shale (510)		
				545 — Ediacara (540-570), Doushantuo Formation (570), Ediacara (605)	545	
PROTEROZOIC	Neo-			Svanbergfjellet Formation (750), Bitter Springs Chert (850)		
				1000	Stromatolites common	
	Meso-			1600		
	Palaeo-			2500	2000	
ARCHEAN				Gunflint Chert/Duck Creek Dolomite (2000)	Banded Iron formations	
				Apex Chert (3460)	3200	
					3500	
				3800 — Oldest sedimentary rocks (3800)	Photosynthesis (carbon isotope evidence)	

above: Timeline highlighting points discussed throughout the text.

based on organic substances known as kerogens. These hydrocarbons are insoluble and are therefore unlikely to be contaminants introduced from rocks of younger age. Chemical analyses also focus on relatively unmetamorphised rocks, because heat and pressure are known to degrade and alter hydrocarbons in many ways, smudging that crucial fingerprint evidence.

One indicator of photosynthesis is the ratio of two isotopes of carbon (^{12}C and ^{13}C) measured in kerogens. Both isotopes are present in carbon dioxide gas, but it has been observed in living plants that the light isotope is preferentially taken up during photosynthesis. This gives plants a higher ratio of ^{12}C than would be expected from background levels. Unlike its radioactive isotope (^{14}C), both ^{12}C and ^{13}C are stable, and their ratio persists in the organic remains of fossils as a physical indicator of photosynthesis. Analyses of kerogens indicates that photosynthesis was well established during the Archean, probably as far back as 3.5 billion years ago, perhaps even to 3.8 billion years ago. This carbon isotope signal is consistent with the presence of cyanobacteria. Some rocks yield more specific indicators of cyanobacteria such as highly resistant molecules that are characteristic of their cell membranes. The derivatives of some of these molecules (e.g. 2-methylhopane hydrocarbons) are found in rocks 2.7 billion years old.

In addition to evidence invisible to the naked eye, the origin of oxygen-producing photosynthesis changed forever the composition and appearance of ancient rocks on a vast scale. Today, the manufacture of steel requires enormous quantities of iron ore, most of which comes from so-called banded iron formations in very ancient rocks (2.0 to 3.5 billion years of age). These iron rich layers contain an abundance of the minerals hematite (Fe_2O_3) and magnetite (Fe_3O_4), which impart a distinctive red colouration to the rock. These oxides of iron formed in ancient seas when molecular oxygen first came into contact with dissolved ferrous iron, oxidising it to the ferric state, at which point it precipitated out of solution as a rusty mist to settle on the sea floor. This process continued on a large scale for nearly 1.5 billion years. It has been estimated that the amount of oxygen locked up in these deposits of iron is roughly 20 times as much as in today's atmosphere. The only microbes to

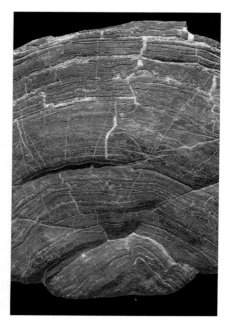

above: Fossil stromatolites, with their characteristic internal banding, are the most visible signs of life in the Proterozoic; *Cryptozoon proliferum,* each measuring approximately 14 cm in width (Proterozoic, New York State, USA).

carry out oxygen-producing photosynthesis are cyanobacteria, so the presence of banded iron formations provides additional geological evidence both for cyanobacteria and for photosynthesis.

IMPRINTS ON THE ROCKS

Thriving and diverse communities of organisms often leave a physical imprint on the environment that remains long after the organisms themselves have gone. The tough carbonate skeletons of corals testify to the ubiquity and diversity of reefs during the Phanerozoic even though the delicate coral polyps have long since vanished through decay. Likewise, in the Proterozoic irregularly shaped mounds called stromatolites provide indirect evidence for microbial communities.

We know from living examples that stromatolites are formed by mat-forming microbes. Cyanobacteria are common to many types of modern stromatolite, where they colonise the surface layers forming an interwoven fabric of thread-like filaments that is flexible but robust. This surface layer overlies further layers of photosynthetic and non-photosynthetic microbes that thrive under oxygen free conditions. Stromatolites grow in response to inundation of the bacterial mat by waves of sediment and mud or through the precipitation of minerals. This causes the mobile cyanobacteria to slough off their mucilagenous sheaths and glide upwards to the new surface, leaving within the body of the stromatolite a tell-tale pattern of layers.

In some stromatolites, the precipitation of calcium carbonate on the growth surface develops into a hard limestone cement, and these rocky forms are common fossils. In fossilised hard stromatolites, the organic remains of the bacterial mat are seldom preserved, but the characteristic thin growth bands do remain. In 1883 Charles Doolittle Walcott – discoverer of the famous Burgess Shale fauna and flora of the Cambrian – reported finding specimens of the fossil stromatolite *Cryptozoon* (Greek for 'hidden life') in strata of Proterozoic age in the Grand Canyon region of the western USA. Since then, it has been recognised that stromatolites are the most abundant macroscopic evidence of life in the Proterozoic.

above: Restoration of Proterozoic ocean floor with bun-shaped stromatolites.

In the Archean, stromatolites are much rarer, and only a handful of examples have been found in rocks older than 3.2 billion years old. The biological origin of some of these ancient forms has been questioned, because it is possible to show that abiotic mineral precipitates could mimic features such as growth bands. There are, however, good reasons for thinking that most fossil stromatolites are biogenic. First, there are the modern analogues in which biological influences can be observed directly. Second, there are examples from the Proterozoic that contain microfossils similar to those in modern forms. Third, the geological distribution of stromatolites in Proterozoic sediments is consistent with a biological origin. Fourth, it is difficult to find stromatolite-like objects that are demonstrably abiotic in the modern world. These distinctive structures are therefore good evidence that menageries of microbes were at work in this early period of Earth history.

Although it is possible in a forensic investigation to establish that a murder has been committed based entirely on circumstantial evidence, the absence of a body is always a worry. Likewise, in the search for early plant life, although there is abundant circumstantial evidence of organisms that are related in one way or another to plant organelles or other biochemical systems, the question inevitably comes back to the organisms themselves. What did they look like, and are they still recognisable? Evidence on the relationships of living organisms indicates that the earliest life forms were microbes. The search for the fossilised remains of early plants therefore has to be conducted on a microscopic scale, and it has focused mainly on carbon rich (black) cherts associated with stromatolites.

Cherts are sedimentary rocks composed of very fine microcrystalline quartz. To examine their contents, one needs to slice them into millimetre-thick slabs, which are then bonded to glass microscope slides and ground to the thickness of a human hair. These so-called petrographic thin sections render the rock translucent, and any organic remains can be studied using high power lenses. The organisms themselves are so minute that if the microscopic search were to be scaled up, it would be the equivalent of looking for pea-pod sized objects on a football pitch that is knee deep in murky water. Each search may require the examination of numerous football pitches, and not all yield results.

Some of the best early microfossil evidence comes from rocks of Proterozoic age. The Gunflint Formation of western Ontario, Canada, and the Duck Creek Dolomite of western Australia yield 2 billion-year-old assemblages of unicells, clusters of unicells, and cellular filaments of various shapes and sizes. Some are very different from known micro-organisms, but others, particularly the filamentous forms, bear a strong resemblance to modern cyanobacteria. In the younger Bitter Springs Chert of central Australia (850 million years old) preservation is so superb that it is possible to relate some microfossils to living

above: Filamentous cyanobacteria from the 850 million-year-old Bitter Springs Formation of Australia. Filament (left) is approximately 20 µm in diameter.

oscillatorian and chroococcalean cyanobacteria. These examples, and data from other localities, provide compelling evidence of diverse communities of micro-organisms in the Proterozoic and the youngest part of the Archean.

Evidence from older rocks is more controversial, either because of poor preservation or through the possibility of contamination by later life forms. Micro-organisms are ubiquitous in sediments and investigators need to establish carefully that the specimens they are working with have not been introduced into the rocks millions of years later. This can occur through cracks and fissures that have subsequently sealed up entombing young organisms in old rocks. One guide is the colour of the fossils themselves. Most Archean rocks have undergone metamorphism to one degree or another. Metamorphism causes the rock to heat up, which makes indigenous kerogen become darker. If micro-organsim contaminants are introduced at a later stage, after metamorphism has long ceased, the colour of their kerogen would be a much lighter brown. One early benchmark, the 3.46 billion-year-old Apex Chert of western Australia, contains cyanobacteria-like filaments, but both their organic and indigenous nature have been questioned. Debates of this sort surround many of the claims of microfossils in the Archean.

The acquisition of mitochondria and chloroplasts by early eukaryotes are events for which there is little direct fossil evidence. We know from comparisons of the structure and molecular biology of living species that these organelles were acquired by eukaryotes through endosymbiosis from alpha-proteo bacteria and cyanobacteria respectively. Even though these momentous microscopic events were not captured in the fossil record, there is good evidence that they had occurred by about 1 billion years ago. We can draw this inference from the fossil evidence because species that are clearly identifiable as eukaryotes based on the recognition of other preserved and more easily observable features are present by this time.

GREEN ALGAE

The green algae are a diverse group of eukaryotes comprising an estimated 8000 living species. These include microscopic unicellular, colonial and filamentous forms, as well as the bright green thalloid plants of seashore and freshwater lakes and rivers. Some are partly or fully enclosed in tough carbonate sheaths. Others are terrestrial, growing on tree trunks, leaves, soil, rocks, and even on permanent snowfields at high altitude. A few live symbiotically with fungi in organisms called lichens, or as photosymbionts in various animals (e.g. *Hydra viridis*).

The search for fossil evidence of green algae is hampered by the fact that diagnostic features are for the most part subcellular or biochemical. Many are also simple and microscopic, and the larger ones usually have flimsy tissue systems that do not lend themselves to preservation. Another difficulty is that frond-like branching systems are widespread in algae and many animal groups, making diagnosis of the affinity of fossils based on this characteristic alone highly problematic. Among the larger fossils that have been attributed to the algae, most are little more than silhouettes on the rocks. The affinities of these shadowy organisms remain controversial and ultimately often indecipherable. In the famous Burgess Shale of Middle Cambrian age, several

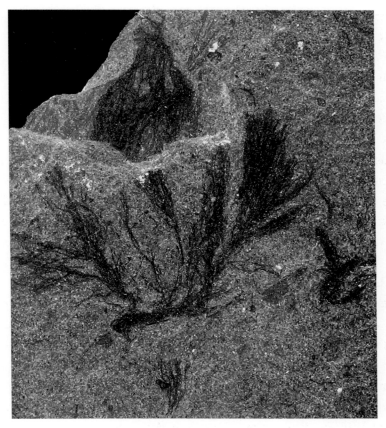

above: Shadows on the rocks: possible filamentous cyanobacteria *Marpolia spissa*, approximately 12 mm in height (Middle Cambrian, Burgess Shale, Canada).

macroscopic branching systems have been attributed to the green algae or other algal groups at one time or another. However, the precise nature of their algal or cyanobacterial affinities remain poorly substantiated.

Just as the possession of carbonate skeletons of one sort or another has saved many groups of invertebrates from geological oblivion, so the fossil history of some green algae has been conserved thanks to an encrusting layer of lime. One of the most prominent of these algae is the Dasycladales, a group that is characteristic of shallow marine seas in warm climates. These plants are for the most part macroscopic, up to 20 cm long, and they have a

above: Encrusting layers of calcium or magnesium carbonate preserving the delicate remains of alga cells of *Coelosphaeridium,* approximately 7 cm in width (Ordovician, Ringsaker, Norway).

distinctive thallus comprising a central stem with branches in whorls. Remarkably, this complex plant body is composed of just a single cell. Many species develop an encrusting layer of lime during their life span, and it is this layer that is found fossilised. The Dasycladales first appear during the middle part of the Cambrian.

The fossil record of green algae is likely to extend beyond the Cambrian into the more ancient Neoproterozoic. Some green algae produce microscopic resting cysts that are extremely resilient. *Tasmanites* is the name for one such fossil that measures about 0.5 mm in diameter. Resting cysts of this type can be common, and they are first recorded in sediments of Late Proterozoic age. Filamentous and thalloid fossils probably attributable to the green algae are well documented in the Neoproterozoic. The phosphatic mudstones of the ca 570 million-year-old Doushantuo Formation of southern China contain exceptionally well preserved algal thalli that might be related to green algae.

Branched filaments, some of which are composed of large cylindrical cells, are known from the 700–800 million-year-old Svanbergfjellet Formation of Spitsbergen. These fossils have been compared to modern green algae in the Cladophorales (Ulvophyceae) and Chaetophorales (Chlorophyceae). In the 850 million-year-old Bitter Springs Formation of Australia, there are microscopic spherical unicells that resemble modern *Chlorococcum* and *Chlorella*. These and other fossil data indicate that green algae had diverged from other eukaryotes by the Late Neoproterozoic, and that some of the major class level groups were already distinct entities by the Middle Cambrian.

GREENING OF THE LAND

The most bizarre and important green algae are the ones that became fully terrestrial. Curiously, these were not the large conspicuous leaf-like marine forms but most probably microscopic freshwater species. Evidence from a variety of sources, including the structure of the plant cell, its biochemical pathways, and more recently its DNA and RNA, show that land plants all share a single origin and that they are most closely related to an obscure group of green algae called the Charophyceae. Living Charophyceae are for the most part unicellular or filamentous algae of lakes and rivers, and most are very simple plants. One consequence of these findings is that it leads us to expect the earliest land plants to be small, simple organisms. The search for early fossil evidence of plant life on land – like the search for early life in the seas – therefore begins in the microscopic world.

The earliest life on land may well have been microbial and algal, and it is possible that terrestrial environments were populated by soil forming microbes long before the ancestors of modern plants moved onto land. There is evidence of soil profiles containing microfossils in sediments as old as 1.2 billion years. By about 470 million years ago, in the Middle Ordovician, the character of microfossil assemblages changed dramatically with the appearance of the first spores. These are microscopic airborne cells that are characteristic of true land plants. Spores and later derivatives such as pollen have highly resistant cell walls containing the phenolic polymer sporopollenin,

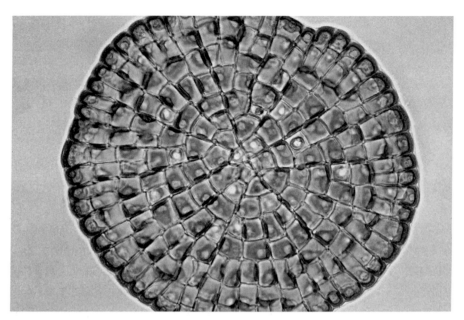

above: The ancestors of land plants were simple microscopic organisms like living *Coleochaete orbicularis*, measuring up to 1 mm in width.

which means that despite their small size they are excellent candidates for fossilisation. Also, they are produced in truly prodigious quantities, and they can be carried by air currents over long distances. These properties of mass production and transport render the spore 'footprint' of a plant much larger than the plant itself. Where spores are found, we know that the parent plant is not far away.

The earliest fossil spores come in a variety of shapes and sizes dubbed monads (single spores), diads (spores dispersed in pairs) and tetrads (groups of four spores). Many are smooth-walled but some possess small spines or processes of one sort or another. Perhaps the most interesting of these spores are the tetrads and those that possess a conspicuous trilete mark on the exterior surface. The configuration of these is indicative of cell division by meiosis, which is a feature of the development of spores and pollen in all land plants. Tetrads, trilete spores and diads have all been documented from *bona fide* fossil land plants. Their presence implies a diverse land flora long before

above: Microscopic spores provide the earliest fossil evidence of plant life on land. Shown here are fossil diad (right) and tetrad (left) spores measuring approximately 35 μm and 40 μm respectively (Ordovician, Arabian Peninsula).

the fossilised remains of the bodies of the plants themselves are first observed.

Alongside the spores are found microscopic scraps of tissue, some of which could represent the decayed and fragmented remains of plants. Sheets of cells resembling the cuticularised and decay-resistant plant epidermis first appear in the Late Ordovician (450 Ma) and become more abundant during the Silurian. These cellular sheets could represent the remains of the waxy cuticle covering the outer surface of a land plant. Wefts of tubes with internal banding are also frequently associated with fragments of cuticle. These enigmatic structures bear a superficial resemblance to tracheids (wood cells) found later in the fossil record. The origins of these fragments is obscure, but an affinity with land plants is possible.

What did the plants that produced the spores and the cuticle fragments look like? There is little direct fossil evidence until about 425 million years ago, some 50 million years after the appearance of the first spores and cuticles. The fossils tell a story

above: Bits and pieces: minute fragments of cuticle and plant parts, approximately 320 μm long, provide additional early evidence of life on land (Lower Devonian, Anglo-Welsh Basin).

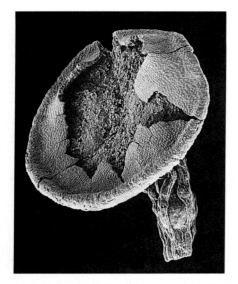 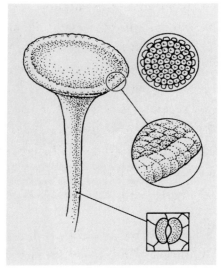

above left: Exquisite preservation of minute spore sac, approximately 1.5 mm in diameter, in charcoal-like substance; *Cooksonia pertoni* (Early Devonian, Shropshire, England).
above right: Interpretative drawing of spore-bearing terminal region of early fossil land plant indicating preservation of such features as spores, epidermal cell pattern and stomata.

of plants that appear very unfamiliar to the modern eye. The earliest known land plants were simple stick-like organisms with bifurcating stems, which probably arose from a prostrate stem-like rhizome. They did not have true leaves and roots. The stem apices terminated in expanded regions of various shapes and sizes. These were the parts that produced the spores. In general terms, the level of structural complexity is comparable to modern day bryophytes, such as the hornwort *Anthoceros*. Although the earliest fossils are rarely preserved as complete plants, it is likely that they were very small, millimetres to a few centimetres in height.

Collecting early land plant fossils is a challenging task that requires patient sifting through much material and careful scrutiny of even the most tiny fragments. The body fossils are commonly simple flattened compressions on the rock in which all of the tissues have been reduced to carbon and the original cell structure destroyed. Occasionally, however, the more resistant structures such as the spores, the waxy cuticular layer covering the epidermis, and the wood are preserved to one degree or another providing valuable information on cellular composition. Fossil plants at most early sites represent terrestrial debris that has been washed into freshwater or shallow-water marine systems. The bits and pieces are disarticulated and are often sorted by size during transportation. Reconstructing whole organisms is a kind of natural jigsaw puzzle in which pieces are often missing. Also, because the plant debris has been transported by water currents, building up a picture of the flora as a whole is not a straightforward business.

THE RHYNIE CHERT

How wonderful it would be to see the world as it was without having to peer through the murky and distorted lens of the fossil record. From time to time, palaeontologists dream of climbing into a time machine that will take them back to their chosen period so that they can witness the past at first hand. If not a time machine, very occasionally science does provide us with a kind of window onto the past that gives a clear and uninterrupted view of the scene. These are sites of exceptional preservation, and they have been dubbed *lagerstatte*, which is a German word meaning 'mother lode' or the main vein of ore in a mine. One of the most important of these is a 400 million-year-old chert from Scotland.

In 1914, Dr William Mackie, a medical practitioner and a member of the Geological Society of Edinburgh, reported finding fossil plants in cherty rocks that had been used to build a garden wall in the remote Scottish village of Rhynie. The source of these rocks was soon located to a neighbouring field. Trenches were dug and fresh subsurface collections made. Mackie gave his specimens to Robert Kidston, a leading expert on the floras of the Carboniferous, who together with William Lang, Professor of Botany at the University of Manchester, England, wrote a detailed account in a series of technical papers published in the *Transactions of the Royal Society of Edinburgh* between 1917 and 1921. The discoveries reported here caused a

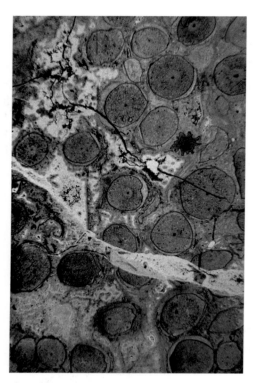

above: Crowded stems of plants in the Rhynie Chert viewed in thin section, approximately 2-3 mm in diameter (Early Devonian, Rhynie Chert, Scotland).

sensation and established the so-called Rhynie Chert as one of the world's most famous fossil sites.

What Mackie had discovered was a complete early terrestrial soil ecosystem with its plants and animals fossilised as they grew. This was by far the earliest and most well-preserved site of its kind, and it remains so. The flora and fauna of the chert include seven land plants, at least six groups of terrestrial and freshwater arthropods, algae, fungi, a lichen and bacteria. The plants are so well preserved in silica, that even the most minute cellular details are faithfully recorded. The fossils are best observed in thin section, and whole plants are reconstructed by the painstaking procedure of making serial slices.

The environment of fossilisation at Rhynie is unusual. The plants grew on or close to a sinter terrace; an extensive formation of silica deposited by a hot spring. This spring periodically flooded its neighbourhood inundating flora and fauna with hot, silica-rich waters. As the water cooled the silica precipitated out entombing and preserving the whole microenvironment in solid rock. Layer after layer of plant-bearing cherts and interbedded sandstones built up in this way. Good modern analogues of the Rhynie Chert would be geyser systems such as those found in Rotorua (North Island, New Zealand) or Yellowstone National Park (USA).

A walk through the Early Devonian landscape at Rhynie would immediately pose a problem to the observer. The tallest plants were slightly short of knee height, and most were much smaller. To fully appreciate the diversity and variety of plants and animals, one would need to crawl on hands and knees equipped with a large hand lens. Like fossils from elsewhere, those from the Rhynie Chert document a world of miniature plants with bifurcating, stick-like stems. Most were leafless, but some bore minute hairs and one had short scale-like leaves. Plants grew in dense clumps, an aspect of growth that probably helped to support an upright posture for their thin stems.

One reason that the Rhynie Chert is such an exceptional site is that plants are preserved with all their soft tissues intact. Cell by cell examination of the interior of the stems is possible. Like their modern counterparts, all of

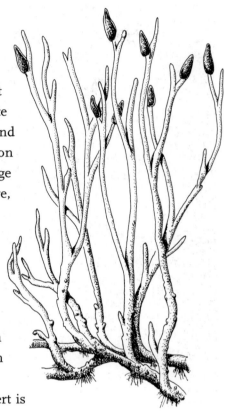

above: Diagrammatic representation of the Rhynie Chert plant *Aglaophyton*, approximately 10 cm tall.

the larger plants had a vascular system that supplied the transpiration stream with water and presumably also facilitated transport of the products of photosynthesis. This tissue system was located at the core of each stem. In general terms, however, the vascular system is much simpler in overall structure and in the details of its individual cellular components than are the equivalent tissue systems of modern land plants. Forming the stem surface was a cuticularised epidermis which bore stomata with characteristic paired sausage-shaped guard cells. Stomata enable plants to take up carbon dioxide

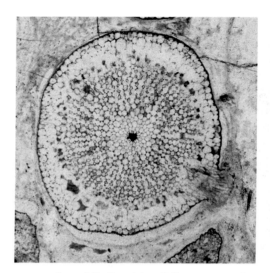 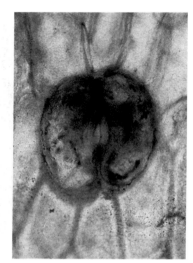

above left: Complete soft tissue preservation at the cellular level in *Rhynia major*. Transverse section through stem, approximately 2 mm in diameter (Early Devonian, Rhynie Chert, Scotland).
above right: Microscopic pores in the plant epidermis facilitate gas exchange with the atmosphere and water transport. The stomata comprise a pair of sausage-shaped guard cells, approximately 60 µm long (Early Devonian, Rhynie Chert, Scotland).

from the atmosphere to fuel sugar production during photosynthesis, while at the same time allowing water to evaporate from the surface thereby drawing up fluids from the basal region. Like most modern land plants, these early fossils would have been able to regulate water loss from the stem surface in times of water shortage by closing down the pore aperture. The airborne spores of the Rhynie Chert plants were borne in tiny purse-shaped or grain-shaped sacs. Taken together, these features demonstrate that the plants were *bona fide* land-dwelling organisms.

An attentive listener at Rhynie with an ear placed close to the ground might well have heard a faint rustling in the undergrowth, because in addition to the plants, the Rhynie Chert is well known for its animals. These were all tiny arthropods. At least six groups are known, and these include miniature predators such as relatives of modern-day spiders (trigonotarbids),

left: Model of spider-like predatory trigonotarbid *Palaeocharinus rhyniensis*, body approximately 5 mm long (Early Devonian, Rhynie Chert, Scotland). below: Mouthparts of *Palaeocharinus rhyniensis* showing a well-preserved chelicera or fang (f) and pedipalp (p). The fang is approximately 300 μm long.

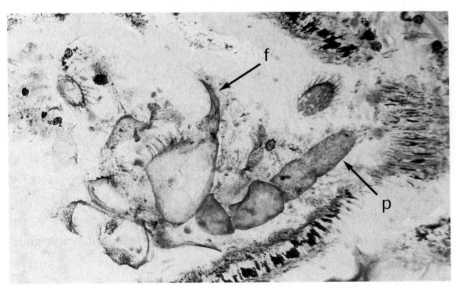

at least one centipede, minute mites, springtails (collembolans), freshwater crustaceans, and an enigmatic extinct group that show similarities to both crustacea and insects (Euthycarcinoids). Although animal remains are much less abundant than plants they too are exceptionally well preserved. The

Rhynie trigonotarbids are among the best known members of this group. Features such as their respiratory organs (book lungs), mouthparts, and even muscle tendons have been observed. Curiously, early land faunas were dominated by voracious carnivores and detritivores (eaters of dead and partly decomposed plants). Eaters of living plants (herbivores) were absent or rare. The nature of this food chain suggests comparisons with modern soil ecosystems.

In addition to providing a glimpse of an Early Devonian world, the plants of the Rhynie Chert confirm the general picture of early life on land emerging from the study of the vastly more common compression fossils, and they add flesh to the bare bones of this story in the form of new information on anatomy, the connection of plant parts and the associations of species with one another.

Evidence from the fossil record shows that the development and integration of the land flora and fauna began from fundamentally different starting points. Early land animals bore a strong resemblance to their aquatic ancestors. They were recognisably arthropod, molluscan or vertebrate, all groups with lengthy aquatic histories stemming from the Cambrian. There were multiple transitions to the land by animals, and each group retained many of the complex organs and tissues found in its aquatic forebears, albeit in modified forms. Adult frogs and fish do not look much alike, but their systems of nerves, blood vessels, skeleton, musculature, early development and basic physiology share much in common because these fundamental systems were inherited from a common ancestor. Not so with plants. When plants moved onto land they took very little in the way of baggage with them. Plants inherited their basic cell biology from green algae, but most of their organs and tissue systems were forged on land. The contrast with animals could hardly be greater. The problems of evolving a terrestrial fauna were solved by tinkering with or fine tuning already complex integrated bodies, each with its own long aquatic history. In plants, however, terrestrialisation witnessed the building of completely new multicellular organisms more or less from scratch.

Once on land, plants interacted principally with the atmosphere, and much of the form and function of these stationary organisms is attuned to this medium. In fact, it has been said that the colonisation of the land by plants is perhaps better termed the colonisation of the air. In water, plants were neutrally buoyant, whereas in air they must be self supporting. On land, water is a limiting factor and plants need to invest in organs that seek it out and conserve it. Propagules – parts such as seeds or spores that detach to form new organisms – need to be light and tough to disperse in air and to survive desiccation. The benefits of life on land include a greater volume of space to expand into than is available in most freshwater systems, and generally higher levels of light intensity for photosynthesis. These new constraints and benefits had huge consequences for the shape of things to come. They played a major part in turning what was an unremarkable group of green algae with a very limited morphological repertoire into one of the most spectacularly diverse groups of organisms on Earth. In the next chapter, we consider some of the consequences for how early groups evolved into the more familiar forms of ferns, conifers and their extinct relatives.

Chapter Two

THE DEVONIAN EXPLOSION
AND ITS CONSEQUENCES

THE FOSSIL RECORD documents the development of life over timescales that are so vast that they are hard to comprehend, difficult to measure, and never known with great precision. Rocks can record events that happened in just hours or days as well as longer-term trends taking place over hundreds of thousands or millions of years. In geology, words such as rapid or sudden take on new meaning, describing events that in human terms would appear to move at a glacial pace. From a geological perspective, the fossil record is full of change. Species come and go, appearing in an instant, lasting for a while, and then vanishing forever. Set against this fluctuating background are periods of more striking change in which life appears to lurch forward producing an abundance of new forms in rapid succession. The most famous of these is the so-called 'Cambrian Explosion' in which multicellular organisms with skeletal hard parts appeared, filling the seas with animal life. Less well known, but arguably just as important, was the burgeoning of life on land during the Devonian. Here, plants were the major players, paving the way for a succession of animal groups.

left: Leafless stems, topped by a cone-like array of spore sacs typified many early land plants, *Protobarinophyton obrutschevii*, stems approximately 3 mm wide (Devonian, north-east Siberia, Russia).

The rocks of the Devonian are where we first begin to see abundant evidence for plant life on land, in the form of fossils visible to the naked eye. It has long been known that plant-bearing rocks of this age can be divided into two broad categories. The older rocks are characterised by small, simple plant fossils, whereas in the younger rocks we find large and highly complex forms. Some of the most striking changes occurred over some 30–40 million years; a comparatively short period in the grand scheme of geological time. During this time the maximum height attained by plants increased some 40 fold, from about 0.5 m to 20 m or more, and there was an enormous increase in the number of species. By the end of the Devonian soils of modern aspect were well developed, forest ecosystems were widespread, and land based animal life was firmly established. In plants, these changes were accompanied by the development of many new organ systems and appendages, as well as a whole new repertoire of reproductive strategies. Few early plants would be familiar to the modern eye, but from within this exotic jumble arose the lineages that gave rise to modern groups such as ferns, conifers and the like. It is groups such as these and their extinct kin that were destined to dominate the land for over 200 million years.

HORSES' TAILS AND WOLVES' FEET

The shapes of plants are often likened to parts of animals, both in popular folklore and in the arcane business of devising Latin names. The famous eighteenth century Swedish naturalist Carl von Linné called his native clubmoss *Lycopodium* (Greek *lukos*, meaning wolf; *podion*, diminutive of *pous*, meaning foot) and the horsetail *Equisetum* (Latin *equus*, meaning horse; *saeta*, meaning bristle, stiff hair). One struggles to see the zoological parallels here, but then as plants go these are simple ones that lack such gaudy accoutrements as flowers. Of these two, the horsetail is perhaps most familiar to gardeners as an invasive weed. This distinctive plant is characterised by stiff, narrow, bristly branches borne in whorls. The confusingly named clubmosses are not in fact mosses at all, even though the two bear a superficial resemblance. Clubmosses are more closely related to ferns and conifers. The 18 or so living species of horsetail and the 1500 species of clubmoss represent a tiny fraction of the modern world flora. Yet, living clubmosses and horsetails are at the very tip of an iceberg of diversity that stretches back over 350 million years. It was the early relatives of these small prosaic plants that dominated the land floras of the Late Palaeozoic.

Clubmosses are the earliest recognisably modern plants in the fossil record. No botanist would have trouble recognising the affinities of extinct *Asteroxylon mackiei*. This fossil plant bore numerous small needle shaped leaves on simple bifurcating stems. Like modern clubmosses the spores were formed in tiny kidney-shaped capsules. Even its anatomy, in particular the shape of the xylem tissues, bore a remarkable resemblance to some modern forms. *Asteroxylon* differs from its living relatives in some important details, but the similarities far outweigh the differences, so much so that this plant would not look out of place in a modern temperate woodland. *Asteroxylon* comes from the 400 million-year-old Rhynie Chert, but there is earlier evidence of clubmosses in rocks of Late Silurian age in Australia (420 million years old). Here flattened compressions of a plant called *Baragwanathia longifolia* bear the characteristic leaves and spore sacs. These early fossils provide evidence of

above: Wax model reconstruction of the fossil clubmoss *Asteroxylon mackiei*, approximately 10 cm tall (Early Devonian, Rhynie Chert, Scotland).

above: Many early plants bore a dense bristly covering of hairs or simple spiny leaves. Stem segment of *Baragwanathia longifolia*, approximately 15 mm wide (Late Silurian/Early Devonian, Victoria, Australia).

the conservation of certain growth forms in plants for remarkable lengths of time.

The allusion to a wolf's paw in the Latin name of the clubmoss comes from the shape of the stems and in particular their dense covering of leaves that resemble tiny bristles. These are one of the most useful diagnostic features in plants of this group, and they are also the earliest examples of leaves in the fossil record. Alongside the leafy clubmosses of the early land floras is another distinctive group of plants called zosterophylls. These are close relatives of clubmosses, resembling them in all features except that they are leafless. The absence of leaves in zosterophylls and in other related fossils implies that the leafy appendages of clubmosses evolved after most of the other distinguishing features of the group. Fossils such as these also demonstrate that leaves were not essential appendages in the early colonisation of the land by plants.

Clubmosses and horsetails constitute less than 1 per cent of living species diversity in plants, but during the Devonian and subsequent Carboniferous, as much as 50 per cent of land plants belonged to these

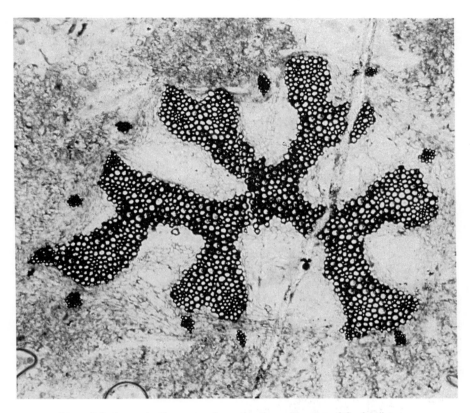

above: Lobed vascular tissue seen in section through a stem of the fossil clubmoss *Asteroxylon mackiei*, approximately 2 mm across (Early Devonian, Rhynie Chert, Scotland). This is one line of evidence for a close relationship between this early fossil and modern clubmosses.

groups and their kin. All modern forms are comparatively small and mainly herbaceous, but by the Late Devonian some clubmosses and horsetails had attained tree size proportions, and these were a significant element of the canopy vegetation in the earliest forests. Both groups achieved their greatest diversity in the coal swamp forests of the Carboniferous.

FERNS AND FEATHERED LEAVES

Designers of solar panels know that the most efficient arrangement of photocells is a flat array that is oriented perpendicular to the Sun's rays.

above: Early relatives of the ferns had branched, blade-less fronds like those of *Protopteridophyton devonicum*, approximately 30 cm long (Late Devonian, Hunan and Hubei Provinces, China).

Such a system enables individual linked cells to access sunlight unimpeded by others. This basic principle has been one of the forces shaping the evolution of leaves, thereby providing a platform for generating an effective solar energy supply in plants. Leaves are very often flat structures with a broad thin blade, which is an ideal configuration for intercepting light. This type of leaf is much more complex than the simple bristles of clubmosses and horsetails. The earliest broad-bladed leaves were of the feathery wing-shaped variety that typifies living ferns.

Above: Partial reconstruction of the habit of the Late Devonian fern-like fossil *Rhacophyton*.

The origins of ferns is a subject that is still shrouded in mystery. The earliest recognisable ferns come from the early part of the Carboniferous, but the origins of the group is certainly earlier still. Devonian fossils such as *Protopteridophyton* and *Rhacophyton* have some fern-like attributes. Like ferns, *Protopteridophyton* and *Rhacophyton* produced spores in small sacs, but these were not organised into special structures (sori) as they are in most modern ferns. Both plants produced large frond-like branching systems, but in comparison to modern fern fronds these were skeletal in appearance. The pinnae and pinnules did not have a proper blade. Instead, the leaf was composed of numerous individual branching elements, which may or may not have been oriented in one plane. These 'proto-fronds' were the functional equivalent of leaves. Fern-like plants such as these were a common element of the Late Devonian landscape.

The complex frond-like branching systems of the fossil plant *Rhacophyton* were undoubtedly a product of the elaboration of simpler dichotomous branching systems. There are many such examples in the

above: Blade-less 'frond' of *Rhacophyton ceratangium*, approximately 9 cm long (Late Devonian, West Virginia, USA).

Devonian. Even earlier relatives of the ferns included plants such as *Psilophyton*. We know that some species of *Psilophyton* had a prostrate rhizome that bore upright leafless branches. The whole plant was probably less than 1 m in height. In some species the main stems bore numerous spine-like outgrowths. Typically, they also bore lateral branch systems that were smaller and more prolifically branched than the main stem.

above: Clusters of rice-shaped spore sacs hang from the side branches of the fossil plant *Psilophyton forbesii*. The stems are approximately 3 mm wide (Early Devonian, Gaspé Peninsula, Canada).

Some of these laterals bore clusters of spore sacs, each the shape of a minute grain of rice, whereas others just terminated in blunt tips. It is thought that lateral branch systems such as these formed the basis for the evolution of a variety of complex lateral appendages in plants, including the feathered-leaf type of ferns.

How could branches possibly evolve into leaves? One leading hypothesis envisages a series of straightforward transformations that could turn a cluster of photosynthetic branches like those of *Psilophyton* into a flat-bladed leaf. Lateral branches grow from the tips. Each tip contains a zone of dividing cells that can either branch to form two new tips, continue to divide to produce stem tissues, or differentiate into a spore sac. Variations in the timing of these events will produce more or less branched laterals. Changes in the orientation of cell division can produce branching that is all in one plane. A combination of increased branching and a change of orientation of cell division could produce a frond-like appendage such as that of *Rhacophyton*. Further cell division along the lateral margins of the branches could produce a web of tissue that joins the individual branching units to form the blade. It is processes along these lines that are thought to have given rise to the feathered leaf type.

above: Partial reconstruction of the fossil plant *Psilophyton crenulatum*, approximately 15 cm in height (Early Devonian, New Brunswick, Canada).
below: From sticks to leaves: possible stages in the evolution of the leaf.

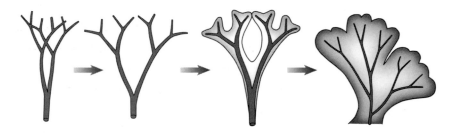

ARCHAEOPTERIS – A BOTANICAL 'MISSING LINK'

The fossil record often throws up organisms with surprising combinations of characteristics that are not seen among living species. Fossils that combine features that are today associated with separate groups are often dubbed 'missing links'. To us they appear bizarre because they bridge gaps in the hierarchy of life that are created by extinction, and the larger the gap the more spectacular the missing link. Missing links tell us about the origins of modern groups and in particular about the sequence in which characteristics were acquired or lost during their evolution. One of the most famous botanical missing links is a plant called *Archaeopteris*. When first discovered, *Archaeopteris* was thought to be a fern, but its true nature was more interesting even though it remained unrecognised for over 100 years.

In 1861, the Canadian geologist Sir JW Dawson illustrated a large fossilised fern-like frond that was known to occur in rocks of Late Devonian age. Dawson called his fossil *Archaeopteris*, a name that bears an uncanny resemblance to the well known fossil bird *Archaeopteryx*. Both words have a similar etymology, being derived from Greek and meaning 'ancient feather or wing', which in the case of *Archaeopteris* is a reference to the size and shape of the leaf. Further evidence of an affinity with ferns came when in 1939 the American palaeobotanist Chester A Arnold discovered that *Archaeopteris* also reproduced by shedding microscopic spores.

Meanwhile, in 1911, an apparently unrelated discovery by the Russian palaeobotanist Mikhail Dmitrievich Zalessky was later to prove significant. Zalessky described a new type of petrified wood from the Donetz Basin, Russia. He called this wood *Callixylon*, and although he did not find any foliage or reproductive structures attached to the trunks, Zalessky noted their similarity to modern conifers. Subsequently, trunks of *Callixylon* were found at many sites throughout Europe and North America, where it is often associated with the fossilised fronds of *Archaeopteris*.

In 1960, almost 100 years after Dawson first described its leaves, the American palaeobotanist Charles B Beck made the unexpected discovery that the foliage (*Archaeopteris*) and the wood (*Callixylon*) were actually part

above: Massive leafy branch of the early tree *Archaeopteris hibernica* was at first thought to be a fern frond. The lower section of the branch bears loose cones containing tiny spore sacs. Approximately 0.5 m of the branch is in view (Upper Devonian, Kilkenny, Ireland).

of the same plant. Here was a plant with fern-like leaves and reproduction borne on a trunk composed of coniferous wood. This particular combination of characteristics is completely unknown among living plants. Beck's observations had led to the discovery of an extinct group of plants that were intermediate between ferns and conifers.

It is now known that *Archaeopteris* was a significant part of the canopy vegetation in the earliest forests. Some species were large trees with substantial trunks that exceeded 1.5 m diameter and 8.5 m in length. In this respect they resembled conifers, but because *Archaeopteris* did not possess seeds, in its reproductive biology it was probably more akin to modern tree ferns. Like its modern analogues, this peculiar early tree exhibited adaptations to light interception and perhaps also to seasonality. The large fronds of *Archaeopteris* seem to have been optimised for light interception. They are composed of numerous smaller leaflets or

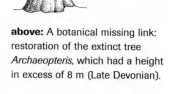

above: A botanical missing link: restoration of the extinct tree *Archaeopteris*, which had a height in excess of 8 m (Late Devonian).

pinnules that in some species are shaped and oriented to avoid shading each other. There is evidence from several species that whole fronds were shed as units, perhaps on a seasonal basis like the leaves of modern deciduous trees. The geological evidence indicates that *Archaeopteris* preferred wet soils, living close to river systems and on floodplains.

Widespread leaf loss could have been associated with seasonal aridity. Leaf loss on a large scale would also have increased leaf litter, which may have accentuated the role of fire in early forest communities.

SEEDS OF SUCCESS

Fruits and the seeds that they contain are among the most varied and economically important plant products. They provide such staples as bread and rice, and our supermarket shelves are laden with all sorts of other kinds that nourish us, enhancing our diet with an almost limitless range of colours, flavours and textures. Seeds are also important because of their place in the plant life cycle. A single seed contains all of the information required to produce an adult plant as well as a compact energy rich reserve of starch to kick-start the embryo. All this is encapsulated in a usually small and relatively light package that can be transported, stored until needed, or indeed eaten.

Seeds were a product of the Devonian Explosion. The earliest seed plants are called pteridosperms (Greek *pteris, pterid*, meaning fern; *sperma*, meaning seed) or 'seed ferns' because their leaves are so similar to those of ferns that it is often impossible on the basis of leaf shape alone to tell the two apart. All seed ferns are extinct, and the fossils are classified into nine groups (six Palaeozoic, three Mesozoic). Some are very well known indeed, whereas our knowledge of others is still very incomplete.

The earliest seed ferns come from sediments of Late Devonian age in northern Europe and North America. These were small shrubs with slender stems. Some are known to have inhabited coastal marshes where they grew in thick, nearly pure stands of vegetation. The fossilised seeds are most often found as isolated parts, due either to post mortem fragmentation or dispersal. Many are readily recognised because they were borne on a deeply lobed structure termed a cupule. The earliest seeds were very small (mostly 3–7 mm in length), and some bore a pair of wing-like flaps protruding from the side. Both features are indicative of dispersal by wind rather than by animal vectors.

One of the major differences between early seeds and those of such modern plants as conifers is that the outer layer of the seed coat – termed the

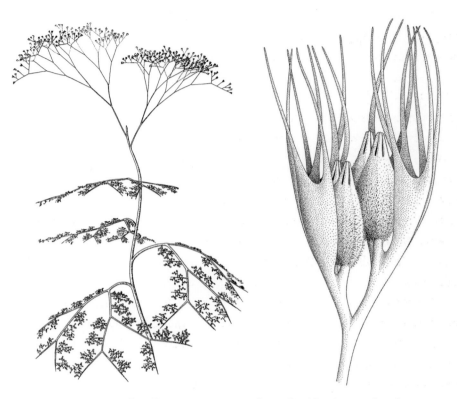

above: Early relatives of conifers were slender shrubs with fern-like leaves, *Elkinsia polymorpha*, approximately 1 m tall (Late Devonian, West Virginia, USA).

above: Seed-bearing cupules of *Archaeosperma arnoldii*, approximately 15 mm long (Late Devonian, Pennsylvania, USA).

integument – is incompletely formed. Like the cupule, it is lobed to varying degrees, whereas in modern conifers the lobes have become fused to produce a continuous outer layer, except for a pore at one end through which the pollen passes. A continuous integument provides seeds with a greater measure of protection from herbivores as well as forming a barrier to water loss, thus helping to keep the delicate internal tissues hydrated. The functions of the lobed cupules and integuments in early seed plants are unknown, but these structures would very probably have affected the pollination biology, which was probably also entirely wind mediated.

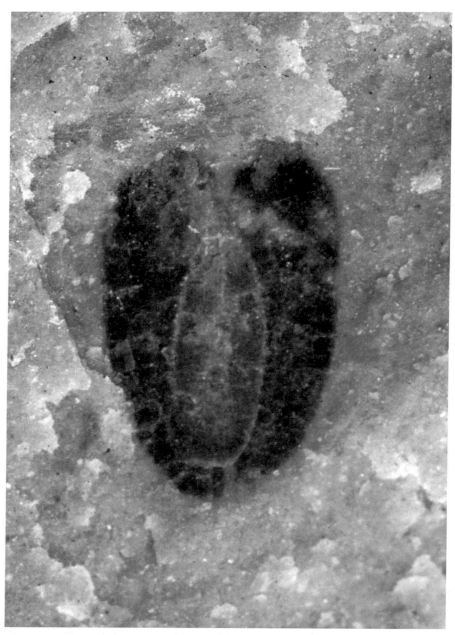

above: At 3 mm in length this tiny winged seed of *Spermolithus devonicus* is barely visible to the naked eye (Upper Devonian, Kilkenny, Ireland).

The evolution of seeds represents a significant shift in the plant life cycle. All land plants possess sexual and asexual phases. In the earliest plants and in such modern groups as ferns and clubmosses these are separate individuals, which usually differ substantially in appearance. However, in seed-bearing plants (e.g. conifers, cycads and flowering plants) the two phases have become bound into a single individual. The sexual phases are reduced to tissues within the seed (technically termed an ovule in its unfertilised state), which are female, and the male gametes that develop from the pollen. Seeds therefore encapsulate the female sexual organs, the fertilisation process and the subsequent developing embryo. By fusing a two-phase life cycle into a single individual, seed-bearing plants have a far greater measure of control over sexual reproduction than do ferns and their kin. They have also developed an enormous range of additional structures that facilitate reproduction (e.g. flowers) and dispersal of progeny in one way or another (e.g. fruit). The evolution of seeds therefore marked a change in life cycle that had far reaching consequences for the biology of plants. In the longer term, the effects of this botanical innovation were felt by other organisms, in particular the many types of animal that feed on fruits and seeds, and those that are involved with the process of pollination.

THE ROOTS OF SOILS

The effects of the Devonian Explosion were most noticeable in the evolution of organ systems such as stems, leaves and seeds – innovations made all the more visible by an accompanying increase in overall size – but these changes above ground were paralleled by an underground revolution of at least equal importance. Roots were also a product of the Devonian Explosion, and these much overlooked organs are one of the most significant innovations in plant life on land. Roots are essential to the development of large plants because they provide a means of anchoring and maintaining an upright posture. Most land plants are literally rooted to the spot. Roots also play a key role in water and nutrient acquisition. More significantly still, *en masse* roots have an incredible impact on the environment. They can break up rock, bind

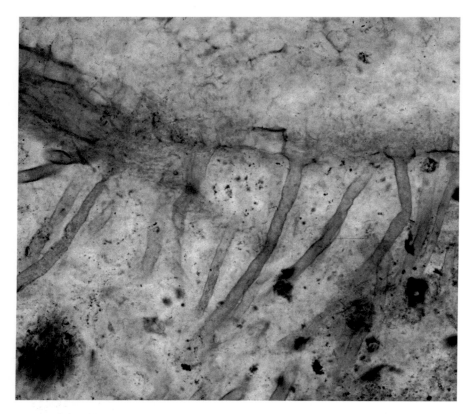

above: Microscopic hair-like absorptive cells on the rooting stems of an early land plant; *Horneophyton lignieri* (Rhynie Chert, Scotland).

loose particles together, and they provide a conduit for the movement of water and solutes, all of which are essential to the development of soils. During the Devonian, plants began to plough, till and fertilise the land, and in so doing they had a lasting influence on the chemistry of the Earth's surface and the atmosphere.

In piecing together a fossil plant to form a conceptual whole it is usually the rooting system that remains the final piece of the puzzle. It is often the case that roots are poorly studied or completely unknown. Although the fossil record of roots is therefore less complete than that of other organ systems, it is possible to discern some general trends. The earliest land

above: Roots and all: rare example of fossil plant with intact rooting system preserved; *Chamaedendron multisporangiatum,* specimen approximately 40 cm long (Late Devonian, Hubei Province, China).

plants, like modern mosses and liverworts, did not have well-developed root systems. These plants bore simple hair-like absorptive cells called rhizoids on prostrate stems and leaves. Some very early fossils are known to have borne branches that appear to be specially modified for rooting. In others, roots were also able to form from dormant buds on aerial stems. Fungi are also known to have played a key role in these early rooting systems, as they do in modern plants. Fungal symbionts have been recorded in the petrified plants of the 400 million-year-old Rhynie Chert, demonstrating a link with mycorrhizal fungi that goes back to the dawn of the land flora. These tiny, shallow rooting systems were adequate for small plants (30–50 cm tall), but larger organisms required something more substantial.

By the Late Devonian and Early Carboniferous an enormous variety of rooting structures had evolved. The evolution of large erect plants, and in particular trees, placed increasing demands upon the anchoring and supply functions of roots. These problems were solved in the main through the development of more extensive underground systems. The evolution of the cambium enabled continuous perennial growth and long term survival of roots in soils. The acquisition of endogenous and adventitious roots permitted repeated penetration of a given soil volume. Roots were also later co-opted to additional functions such as buttresses or mantles in the formation of trunks in ferns and as holdfasts in epiphytes and climbers.

One important consequence of all this was that there was a progressive and ultimately massive increase in root biomass during the Devonian, which had an enormous impact on the development of soils. Prior to the Devonian, soils, if developed at all, are thought to have been predominantly thin and of microbial origin. By the Middle Devonian soil penetration depths of roots were still shallow (less than 20 cm), but this increased to 1 m or more as forests spread. The diversity of soils also increased. This change was brought about by root induced weathering and mixing. By the end of the Devonian there was an increase in soil clay content, structure and profile maturity that correlated with increases in the depth of root penetration. Soils with modern profiles are recognisable at this time.

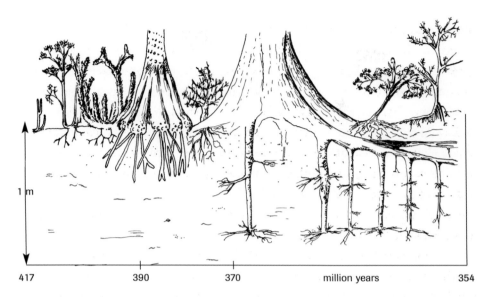

1 m

417   390   370   million years   354

above: Diagram depicting changes in complexity and depth of penetration of soils by roots through the Devonian.

The impact of roots on the environment extends beyond their immediate effects on the development of soils. The presence of roots in soils increases the natural weathering of calcium and magnesium silicate minerals. This apparently mundane fact turns out to have extremely important consequences for climate and temperature globally. Under natural circumstances, calcium and magnesium silicates react chemically with a dissolved form of the gas carbon dioxide, which comes from the atmosphere. This produces soluble calcium and magnesium carbonates, which are transferred through the groundwater system to rivers and ultimately to the oceans, where they are precipitated out as limestone and dolomite. Across the surface of the Earth, these chemical reactions occur on a vast scale, removing carbon dioxide gas from the atmosphere and locking it up as carbonate in rock formations. This reduces the so-called greenhouse effect, which leads to lower global temperatures. In other words the widespread development of roots in land plants affected the chemistry of the atmosphere and the oceans, which summed over millions of years adds up to changes in climate on a global scale.

DEVONIAN FLORAS

The rocks of the lower part of the Devonian provide the first glimpse of plant life on land on a global scale, based on samples from numerous sites. Most of these fossil-bearing deposits were laid down in lakes, river systems or nearshore shallow-water marine deposits. They document for the most part wetland habitats from the tropical or subtropical regions. The data accrued over many years tell a tale of early communities that were simple in structure with low species diversity. The form of plant growth had a major influence on community structure. Most plants were rhizomatous, which means that prostrate stems spread out along the ground giving rise periodically to upright aerial branches. Individuals could therefore be quite large in the horizontal dimension – they could cover a large area of ground – but they were short in stature, for the most part less than 2 m in height. Because of this, plants tended to grow in dense but patchy stands that were dominated by a single species. All were herbaceous and had branched stick-like stems. Most were leafless, but leaves where present were all short and spine-like in shape. The dense shading provided by broad leaf canopies characteristic of later floras was completely absent. Sampling of plant communities for the early part of the Devonian, although global in scale is still sparse, so it is difficult to make well-substantiated statements regarding the character of the flora in different parts of the world. Certainly a degree of endemism has been recognised, but this is not particularly marked compared with younger geological periods.

As we pass up through the Devonian, the change in the nature of plant life on land is perhaps more radical than at any other period of geological time. By the latter part of the Devonian there were more species of plants in a greater number of environments than there had ever been, plants had increased massively in size with the development of the tree habit, they had evolved a wide variety of additional organ systems such as wood, roots and leaves, and there had been an elaboration of the basic life cycle in several directions, including the evolution of reproduction by seeds. Forested areas had become common, and there were clear habitat distinctions among plants. One can recognise stratified communities that comprise such familiar elements as canopy-forming trees, understories composed of shrubs and herbaceous ground cover (see p. 67). It is also possible to discern different habitats with their own characteristic floras. Deposits from Arctic Norway and the eastern seaboard of the USA document the earliest evidence of peat forming wetlands. Peat swamps were dominated by the fern-like plant *Rhacophyton*, and these wetter areas were fringed by tree clubmosses. Stream-side habitats were home to stands of the plant *Pseudobornia*, an early relative of modern horsetails. Poorly drained soils supported low diversity forests of large *Archaeopteris* trees. In better drained areas of the floodplain *Archaeopteris* forests flourished with a variety of understory shrubs, including seed-bearing forms and fern relatives, as well as clubmosses and early vining plants.

The echoes of the Devonian Explosion can be felt to the present day, in the basic unity of the fundamental organ systems of plants and in the multitude of different groups that can trace their origin back to common Devonian stock. By the end of the Devonian, land based animal life was also well established. The Earth was crawling with small animals including mites, millipedes and springtails, scorpions and pseudoscorpions, spiders and centipedes of one sort or another, as well as extinct fish-like vertebrates the size of small dogs. These developments, coupled with the revolution in the soil and the advent of forests, saw the onset of terrestrial ecosystems of more modern aspect. The interactions of plants and animals – at first distant and ill defined – gradually became a driving force behind the evolution of life on land. The Devonian has been called the golden age of plant evolution. Some of the consequences are explored in more detail in the following chapters.

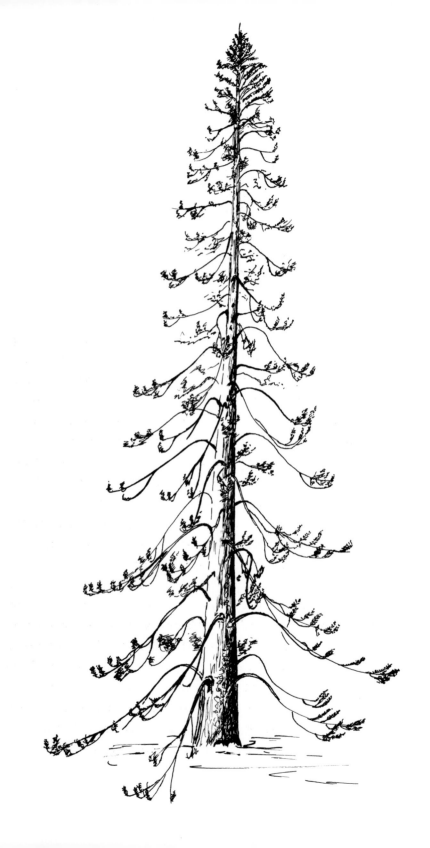

Chapter Three

FORESTS
· · · · · · · · · · · ·

THE CLEARING OF FOREST to create space for agriculture and building
is one of the hallmarks of the growth of human societies, and the impact of
this phenomenon has been so great that it is easy to overlook the importance
of forests in the ecology of the Earth. Forests of many and varied types are
natural and ubiquitous elements of the land flora in all but the most arid and
cold regions. Today, rainforest makes up almost half of the tree covered area
of the planet, and it is home to more species of plants and animals than all
other land areas combined. Temperate deciduous forest and coniferous forest
cover huge swathes of territory in the northern hemisphere, where climate
and season combine to enforce periods of dormancy for many plants during
the winter. An open canopy is more typical of the savanna of semi-arid
regions. Here, grasses predominate alongside scattered broad leafed and
evergreen trees or shrubs. These and other distinctive forest types are
characteristic of particular regions, but forest distribution and composition
have not been static over geological time. Major changes of vegetation were
in fact the norm, driven by factors such as climate change, shifting continents
and the evolution of new species. The fossil record documents these changes and
demonstrates that forests have been an integral part of the vegetation of the Earth for almost as
long as plants have lived on land.

left: Artist's depiction of
Araucarioxylon arizonicum,
the dominant conifer of
Petrified Forest National
Park, Arizona, USA
(Late Triassic).

FAMOUS FOSSIL FORESTS

When trees are killed *en masse* and are rapidly buried in sediment their trunks and other parts can become fossilised to preserve a record of forests written in stone. Frequently, but not exclusively, fossilisation of forests is associated with violent volcanic eruptions. These natural catastrophes can envelop large areas in clouds of fine ash, which kills trees and partly buries them still rooted to the spots where they grew. Sometimes volcanic activity is so violent that it will knock over and entomb thousands of trees simultaneously. This can occur when forests are blasted by pyroclastic flows (fast moving clouds of lethal hot volcanic ash and rock) or lahars (mudflows composed of volcanic debris). Under circumstances such as these, trees are preserved as horizontal logs that may have been transported some distance from their sites of growth. The area of forest fossilised varies enormously from just a handful of tree trunks to many thousands of trunks covering thousands of hectares of land.

Hundreds of such forests are known, and they are found on all continents, including Antarctica. These unique fossil sites have much to tell us about the evolution of Earth's flora, and they are important for tracking changes of a broader nature, such as variations in climate at local and global levels. These most remarkable of natural phenomena can also be appreciated for their aesthetic qualities; the beauty of the fossil wood and the natural wonder of forests turned to stone.

Fossil forests have been known for hundreds of years, but in the seventeenth century the existence and formation of petrified tree trunks was puzzling. Federico Cesi (1585–1630),

above: Fossilised tree trunks of Pliocene age at Dunarobba, Italy.

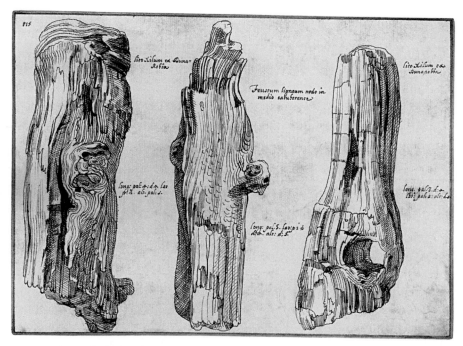

above: Seventeenth century pen-and-ink drawing of three pieces of fossil wood from Dunarobba, Italy

Duke of Acquasparta and founding member of l'Accademia dei Lincei – modern Europe's first scientific society – was one of the first to make a serious scientific study of a fossil forest. As a young man, Cesi's attention had been captured by some strange woods protruding from the ground in various places on his estate in Italy. These woods proved to be the fractured and broken trunks of dead trees. They bore no leaves or fruits, but most remarkably the wood itself had partly turned to stone or in some cases had a metallic appearance. Cesi noted that these woods had other properties too. Some specimens glowed in the dark; others heated up when moistened with cold water. More unusual still, subterranean fires smouldered at some sites, giving off acrid sulphurous fumes.

What exactly were these mysterious woods and how did they form? Cesi and his contemporaries were absorbed by this question because it seemed relevant to several key scientific issues of the day, in particular the nature of heat and light, and the relationship between living things and minerals. After documenting the woods in enormous detail through accurate drawings and struggling mightily with various ideas on how they might have formed, Cesi was unable to decide whether the petrified wood represented once living trees that had turned to stone or stones that were in the process of becoming wood!

This scientific study of the petrified forest known as Dunarobba in the Umbrian Hills, Italy, was the first of its kind, and it illustrates how renaissance scientists struggled to understand the nature of fossil forests. We now know that in geological terms Dunarobba is comparatively young. The sediments are of Pliocene age (1.8 to 5.3 million years old). Currently exposed there are at least 40 closely spaced upright trunks. These substantial trees measure 0.5–2.5 m in diameter and up to 10 m in height. Preservation ranges from true petrifactions in various iron minerals to lignites, which are formed from wood that is hardly mineralised at all. Typically, the tree composition of fossil forests differs from that in the contemporary flora of the region, and Dunarobba is no exception. Here the main fossil species belong to the redwood family (Taxodiaceae) and are thought to be related to the Coastal Redwood (*Sequoia sempervirens*) of the western USA and *Glyptostrobus pencilis* of southern China. Nowadays, the redwoods are confined to south east Asia, North America, and Tasmania. Dunarobba provides direct evidence that this family was also part of the European flora in the relatively recent geological past.

In the nearby site of Rosaro, the mysterious underground fires noticed by seventeenth century writers were actually fuelled by fossil trees. Some of these fires may have started spontaneously. Curiously, the ignition source might even have been one of the petrifying agents. Iron pyrite or fool's gold is an iron sulphide mineral commonly found in fossil wood where it is often the main agent of petrifaction. Pyrite oxidises rapidly on contact with air and water, and this reaction is exothermic. Hence Cesi's observation that certain woods became warm on contact with moisture. Under certain conditions, this chemical reaction can generate enough heat to cause ignition of organic material. Lignites within the ground have also been set alight inadvertently by humans, with spectacular results. One Italian writer reported that a small camp fire built by local shepherds ignited the soil leading to an underground conflagration which burned for seven years!

Fossil forests are sometimes found in parts of the world where few plants grow today. These provide evidence of changing climates in the distant past. In Strathcona Fiord, Ellesmere Island (Canadian Arctic), there is a forest of large standing tree stumps preserved as petrifactions by the mineral calcite (calcium carbonate). The stumps are conical, up to 1.8 m tall, with roots spreading up to 5 m. The trees were closely spaced with an estimated 367 stumps per hectare. All are conifers in the redwood family Taxodiaceae. Geological studies indicate that they grew in freshwater, swampy conditions in waterlogged peat. Fossilisation occurred through the natural periodic shifting of river channels, burying stumps under silt and sand. The Strathcona Fiord forest is Eocene in age, and is thought to be some 50 million years old. This fossil forest provides evidence of a mild temperate climate with high rainfall at a latitude beyond 70°N, well into the present day Arctic Circle.

above: Arctic forest: Geodetic Hills, Axel Heiberg Island, Canadian Arctic Archipelago (Eocene). Unlike the forest at Strathcona Fiord, the wood in these stumps is relatively unaltered.

above: Forest upon forest: a total of 27 petrified forests lie buried in as much as 2000 feet of sediments at Specimen Ridge, Yellowstone National Park, USA. The fossilised trees are over 50 million years old.

Evidence of climatic change can also come from comparisons of living forests and fossil forests from the same region. In Yellowstone National Park, USA, there is a remarkable series of 27 fossil forests stacked layer upon layer through some 366 m of sediment. At the famous Specimen Ridge site, the forest layers are exposed on a hillside. Each layer preserves trees rooted in their original positions of growth. This series of forests was again formed during the Eocene, approximately 50 million years ago, by successive periods of volcanic activity interspersed by periods of quiescence. During active volcanism, massive amounts of debris were ejected form a nearby volcano and deposited on the forest. This debris killed the trees and other plants and partially buried the tree trunks, resulting in the formation of petrified stumps up to 4.5 m tall entombed in layers of ash and other debris. During periods of quiescence, new soil layers eventually formed on top of the buried forest and a new forest of living trees developed. By counting the annual growth rings in the petrified wood, it is possible to show that some of these forests grew for 500 years or more before they were again subject to another period of volcanic activity. In this way, layer upon layer of fossil forests developed. More than 80 kinds of trees, shrubs and herbs are known. The most abundant of these are planes, walnuts, magnolias, chestnuts, oaks, redwoods, maples, persimmons, dogwoods, laurels and bays. The flora also contains exotics such as the oriental katsura tree (*Cercidiphyllum*) and the east Asian Chinquapin (*Castanopsis*). The tree composition of the fossil forest is typical of warm-temperate to subtropical floras, whereas the modern forest of this area contains species characteristic of cool temperate to subarctic environments. A comparison of the fossil with the modern therefore indicates significant climatic cooling. This is probably due to a combination of factors including a generally warmer Earth during the Eocene and the higher elevations of the Yellowstone Park today.

Moving further back in time into the Jurassic and Triassic, one is immediately struck by the dominance of conifers as canopy trees in forests and the complete absence of flowering plants. Some of the petrified forests of the Mesozoic are also of enormous size and contain fossilised tree trunks

above: Fossilised tree trunks scattered over large areas of the Colorado Plateau mark the remains of forests fossilised over 210 million years ago (Petrified Forest National Park, Arizona, USA).

of truly gigantic proportions. The Petrified Forest National Park, Arizona (USA), covers 37,700 hectares of the Colorado Plateau. The Cerro Cuadrado petrified forest in Patagonia is of comparable size. In both areas the ground is strewn with thousands of enormous silicified tree trunks. In Arizona, so common are the trunks that in the sixteenth century, native Americans built a house entirely out of fossilised trees (Agate House). In both Arizona and Patagonia most trunks are horizontal, and many are very large indeed. In the Cerro Cuadrado some can approach 3 m in diameter and nearly 50 m in length. Fossil wood from these areas is also renowned for the beauty of its colours, and it is much sought after by collectors. The beautiful fossilised cones of the Cerro Cuadrado petrified forest are widely found in fossil collections throughout the world. The forest in Arizona dates from the late part of the Triassic (210–227 million years old), whereas the Patagonian forest is probably younger, dating from the Middle to Late Jurassic (142–180 million years old). The dominant trees in both areas were conifers in the Monkey-Puzzle family

above: Cones turned to stone: silicified cones of *Araucaria mirabilis*, approximately 7 cm in size (Late Jurassic, Cerro Cuadrado petrified forest, Santa Cruz, Argentina). Small heavy cones such as these have been used as weights in 'bolas', a type of hunting weapon. Three cones were sewn into leather sacks which the hunter threw around the prey's neck to strike the jugular vein.

(Araucariaceae). In Patagonia, *Araucaria mirabilis* is the predominant tree, and this extinct species is thought to be most closely related to living *Araucaria bidwilli*, the 'bunya bunya' from Queensland, Australia. Evidence such as this demonstrates that Araucariaceae are an ancient family that were much more widespread and diverse during the Mesozoic.

The most ancient forests are found in the Late Palaeozoic. Many of the plants of this period belong to groups that are now extinct, and much research has gone into understanding their structure and biology. Much of the information that enables us to piece together these

above: The Monkey-Puzzle family (Araucariaceae) was a prominent element of ancient forests of the Mesozoic Era. Norfolk Island Pine (*Araucaria heterophylla*).

ancient giants comes from petrified forests. One of the most famous Palaeozoic forests lies underneath the city of Chemnitz in Saxony (Germany). This forest first became known as a source of precious stones. The archdukes of eighteenth century Saxony had expensive tastes, and they maintained splendid collections of jewellery and gemstones. In 1740, David Frenzel, an official employed to scour the country for high quality specimens, discovered several large petrified tree trunks in the suburb of Hilbersdorf. These were transported to Dresden where they were cut and polished to embellish jewellery boxes. As more trunks were found it became apparent that they were of scientific significance. In 1832, Heinrich Cotta showed that the fossil trees were quite different in structure to those of the modern German flora. The fossil flora includes exotic tree ferns, extinct groups related to conifers, and horsetails of tree size proportions. The trunks of some tree ferns are remarkably slender, attaining a height of 12 m but rarely exceeding 35 cm in diameter. These fossils document a series of exotic tropical environments from the Permian, 260–290 million years ago.

Some fossil forests are important sources of fuel in the economies of the modern world. All coal is the fossilised remains of plants, and in Britain most coal is of Late Carboniferous age (290–323 million years old). Within coal seams, compaction renders most plants unrecognisable, but in associated clays and sandstones the leaves and stems are often preserved. In the late 1880s, excavations to create a path in Glasgow's Victoria Park unearthed a small fossil forest of Carboniferous age. Although modest by comparison with subsequent finds, this discovery is significant due to the exceptional preservation of the external form of the tree trunks and because it happened within sight of the Clyde River, one of the great industrial centres of the Victorian era. At the time, the burgeoning industrial revolution and the economic strength of the Clyde were fuelled by coal produced from trees such as these. The significance of this discovery was not lost on the inhabitants of the city, who paid for the construction of a small building to cover the site and to preserve this petrified forest. A total of 11 erect stumps were found, some of which display in a spectacular fashion the large prostrate root systems that

above: The bases and roots of giant clubmoss trees from Fossil Grove, Glasgow, Scotland (Carboniferous).

characterised the giant extinct clubmoss trees. The so-called Fossil Grove of Victoria Park in Glasgow provides insights into the structure and distribution of trees in one small corner of a coal swamp forest.

The oldest fossil forests come from the Devonian. Rocks of this age are particularly well exposed in parts of eastern North America and Canada. In the autumn of 1869 a flash flood tore out bridges, culverts and roads near the small village of Gilboa in the Catskill Mountains. The force of the water was such that sections of a creek were washed away to reveal a small fossil forest. The tree stumps are curiously shaped with bulbous bases and roots radiating outwards like the spokes of a wheel. Closer inspection shows that these are sandstone casts of the original trunks, and even though they are small (less that 0.5 m in diameter and 1 m tall) a modest specimen can easily weigh 100 kg. Geological interpretations indicate that the Gilboa plants grew in a waterlogged soil formed in a coastal or estuarine setting. There is evidence that the trees were killed catastrophically through inundation by sand. The bases of the trunks were initially buried to a depth of 1 m. Death followed quickly, and they rotted leaving natural moulds of the trunks. Later, the decayed bases were filled in by another wave of sand to produce natural sandstone casts. Because only the bases are preserved and there is no wood structure remaining, the affinities of these plants is controversial. They are most likely relatives of the giant lycopod trees that were to dominate the forests of the Carboniferous. The fossil forest at Gilboa holds a special place in the history of plant life because at 375 million years old, it is the oldest in which substantial standing trunks are preserved.

THE FIRST FORESTS

The ancient petrified trees at Gilboa provide unequivocal evidence that forests were already a feature of the terrestrial landscape at an early stage

above: Fossil tree stump, approximately 0.5 m in diameter from oldest-known forest, Gilboa, New York State, USA (Middle Devonian, about 375 million years old).

in the history of plant life on land. But how did trees themselves evolve? We have seen how the earliest land flora consisted of small herbaceous plants that seldom exceeded 1–2 m in height. By the middle of the Devonian – some 380 million years ago – two key innovations in the structure of the plant body paved the way for the development of trees. The first of these was the evolution of roots. These underground organs serve to anchor plants firmly to the soil, and they provide a means of meeting the great demands for water and essential minerals imposed by large plants. The second was the evolution of the cambium: a region of dividing cells around the circumference of stems and roots that enables plants to increase in girth. This provided a mechanism for adding strengthening tissues to create a sturdy trunk that could support

above: Artist's depiction of a Late Devonian landscape: giant clubmosses and horsetails dominated the earliest forests, alongside early relatives of the ferns and gymnosperms.

a large crown of branches. These and other innovations increased the maximum size attainable by plants by more than an order of magnitude. The effect was a rapid change from a world of waist high vegetation to one in which woody giants predominated.

Viewed from a distance, the earliest forests would have provided a reassuringly modern feel to the Palaeozoic world, but on closer inspection this is quickly seen to be an illusion. In the modern world, the canopy element is composed mainly of conifers and flowering plants. These were completely absent from the earliest forests. Here instead we find unfamiliar groups such as giant clubmosses and horsetails, whose living relatives are all herbaceous. Alongside these were groups such as progymnosperms; extinct plants that sported fern-like foliage on a woody trunk. In these early forests the ancestors of modern conifers and flowering plants were small shrubs that were well and truly part of the understory. Other elements of the understory included herbaceous clubmosses and plants related to ferns. The plants themselves differed substantially from modern groups in important aspects of their form and biology. Few species had true leaves. In many, the main platforms for photosynthesis were stems, finely divided stem-like branching systems, or long grass-like appendages. Unlike modern conifers and flowering plants, none of the large trees reproduced by seed. All had a method of reproduction more akin to that in ferns. The earliest forests therefore possessed the key structural elements of canopy tree, woody shrub, and herbaceous understory, but these familiar roles were filled by unfamiliar plants with a form and biology that differs significantly from those in the forests of today.

DIFFERENT WAYS TO MAKE A TREE

In the scramble for the sky that seems to have characterised the Late Devonian landscape, plants converged on several different ways to make a tree. This iterative convergence on a particular form of growth among distantly related species provides strong circumstantial evidence for adaptive evolution. One plausible selection pressure favouring the evolution of trees is competition for light. Small plants growing together shade each other, reducing the quality of light available for photosynthesis. Benefits accrue to those individuals who are taller than their neighbours. The tree habit brings other benefits of greater size, including longevity and the ability to produce larger numbers of spores or seeds and therefore potentially more offspring.

One key element in making a tree is the trunk. Tree trunks need to be strong enough to bear a crown of branches and leaves but flexible enough to withstand the sheering effects of wind. From the standpoint of efficient use of energy and resources, a good trunk should require little in the way of maintenance and it should be as cheap as possible to construct. Also, it must self-assemble and be fully functional throughout its development. During the Late Palaeozoic, plants hit upon several different ways to solve the engineering problems posed by trunks.

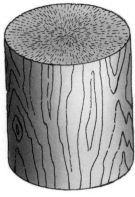

dense wood of conifer

tough outer cylinder encasing soft
interior of tree clubmoss (extinct)

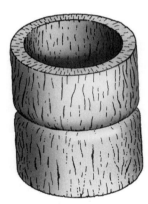

hollow trunk of tree horsetail (extinct)

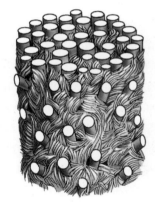

fibrous composite trunk of tree fern

above: Different ways that trees solved the problem of making a trunk.

In most trees, trunks are woody cylinders. These solid trunks are typical of modern conifers and their Palaeozoic relatives. In trunks of this type the xylem tissue has been recruited to play a crucial role in structural support. This tissue has properties that make it ideally suited to stiffening trunks. Xylem cells function as an interconnected system of tubes for conducting water throughout the plant body. These cells actually die and lose their protoplasm before they become functional, and they are endowed with a thick cell wall that is impregnated with a complex chemical compound (an organic polymer) called lignin. This makes the cell walls waterproof and very stiff. Wood is formed through the continual addition of xylem cells to the interior and bark to the exterior. Trunks formed in this way are solid cylinders that are highly resistant to buckling, and they are easily formed and added to during the development of the individual plant. The main disadvantage of a trunk of this type is that it requires a lot of material in the form of wood. In terms of resource usage, it is expensive to build. However, plants with solid trunks can branch profusely and develop a large crown.

A second type of trunk – the hollow trunk – is typical of the tree horsetails of the Palaeozoic, but this form of construction is very rare in modern trees. Tree horsetails developed a ring of woody tissue around hollow interior chambers to produce a kind of reinforced tube. The hollow cylinder forms a good trunk because it concentrates strengthening tissues at the periphery, which is by far the most effective place. Hollow trunks provide maximum stiffness at minimum cost. Plants with this type of trunk are also fast growing. The disadvantage of hollow trunks is that they are sensitive to local buckling at branching points. So, trees of this type usually have small, sparsely branched crowns with small branching angles.

A variant on the hollow trunk is seen in the extinct tree clubmosses, which are thought to have reached heights of up to 40 m with trunks reaching 2 m diameter at the base. These plants possessed a small inner core of woody tissue surrounded by a wide zone of living parenchyma cells. But here again the main support tissue developed as a ring around the circumference. This tissue was produced from a cambium and was lignified, but unlike conifers these cells were not involved in water transport. In tree clubmosses, the roles of water conduction and structural support became decoupled. Trunks of this type had a hard outer surface surrounding a soft interior. A broadly similar sort of construction has evolved independently in living cycads, but different tissue systems are involved. As with the hollow trunk of horsetails, plants with this type of trunk anatomy generally have small, sparsely branched crowns.

A third way to make a trunk is to bind together numerous isolated strengthening elements to form a kind of buttressed or braced trunk. The first group to hit upon this constructional principle was the ferns, but a broadly similar approach using different tissue systems also evolved in some extinct gymnosperms and later in palms. In tree ferns, one or more stems are buttressed by a thick mantle of leaf petioles and roots. Because roots grow downward from the apex, the root mantle (buttress) is thickest at the base of the trunk. The trunks of tree ferns are strong, very lightweight, fibrous and able to absorb and retain rainwater for crown growth. Because trunks of this type have isolated but cross-linked strengthening elements they are more sensitive to bending and to forces acting perpendicular to the long axis of the trunk. This means that the trunks of tree ferns do not generally branch much, and they produce smaller trees that are more suited to the understory where they have a measure of protection from wind.

The evolution of tree trunks therefore involved the co-option of a variety of existing tissue systems and organs to new roles in structural support. Plants made use of structures as diverse as water-conducting cells, the petioles of old leaves and even roots. Individually or in combination, all of these can be produced in ways that add to the girth of the trunk, increasing its strength throughout the plant's life. During the Palaeozoic, strengthening elements were deployed to produce solid, hollow and buttressed or braced trunks. Each trunk type had different mechanical properties, and each represented a solution to the problem of gaining height. The mechanical properties of trunks also affected and set limits on the overall shape and size of trees.

WOOD TURNED TO STONE

Unlocking the intricate details of trunk anatomy in ancient trees to observe the nature of the trunks themselves and to identify the tree species is possible because of the exquisite preservation of details down to the cellular level. The reason that cellular preservation is common in fossil plants but rare in fossil animals lies in the nature of the plant cell wall. The cells of all organisms are bound by a thin semi-permeable membrane that regulates the exchange of materials between the cell interior and its environment. In plants there is an additional much thicker and more robust external layer called the cell wall. This is composed mainly of cellulose fibres, which in some tissue systems such as wood become encrusted with an organic polymer called lignin. This additional wall layer makes plant cells highly robust and resistant to decay. These are properties that make wood a useful building material, and they also enable plant cells to withstand the rigours of petrifaction, providing palaeobotanists with a wealth of data on the internal structure and cellular systems of ancient plants.

Wood is one of the plant tissues most frequently preserved in the fossil record. It sometimes occurs in non-mineralised form in peats, lignites, coals and jet. Petrifaction is also common, and there are more than 40 known minerals of widely diverse chemical affinity that can act as petrifying agents. Of these, the most common is silica, but petrifactions also frequently form in calcium or magnesium carbonates and iron minerals, such as the iron sulphide known as pyrite or fool's gold. Preservation can be so perfect that at a glance one is unable to tell apart a real tree trunk from a fossil that may be over 100 million years old.

For common silica petrifactions to form, wood needs to be saturated with water containing silica in a soluble form. In nature, these conditions are commonly met in volcanic terrains where explosive volcanism has blasted enormous quantities of fine silica-rich ash into rivers and lakes and felled large numbers of trees. The process of silicification is not fully understood, but it is thought to begin through the selective removal from solution of silicic acid monomers through hydrogen bonding with cellulose fibres in the cell wall. As concentrations of these monomers build, they begin to interact and polymerise, depositing films of amorphous silica. Slowly, over millions of years, the amorphous silica is transformed into tiny, tightly packed silica spheres called opal, or a fibrous or ultra-fine micro-crystalline quartz known as chalcedony. The end point of this process is a petrified tree trunk, which typically contains more than 90 per cent by weight of silica. Although silicified woods are often so perfectly preserved that they look modern, their true nature is revealed on touch. They are always very hard, they feel colder than wood, and, typically they are five times heavier.

In addition to their scientific value, silicified woods are prized by collectors for their ability to hold a fine polish and for the beauty of their colours. Here, coloration is more important than the details of cell structure. In fossil woods, coloration occurs in two completely different ways. Most colours are pigments that originate as salts or trace elements such as iron (ferrous or ferric), copper, cobalt and manganese. More rarely – in precious opal and some forms of chalcedony – colours also form through the diffraction of light. Here, regular packing of uniform microscopic spheres of silica (opal) or fine banding of quartz fibres (chalcedony) act like an interference grating. Light falling on the surface of the fossil is diffracted into a rainbow of colours. This is the source of the vibrant coloration observed in precious opal and rainbow agates.

MATCHING THE WOODS TO THE TREES

Reconstructing the vegetation of fossil forests frequently entails the identification of species based on wood anatomy. The process of wood identification is more or less the same for living and fossil woods, but it is a tricky business that is highly technical and time consuming. Identification involves the use of specialist wood keys, which are based mainly on microscopic characteristics of tissue structure. Petrified wood must be carefully prepared for microscopy by grinding to thin slivers for translucent minerals (e.g. silicates) or polishing for opaque minerals (e.g. pyrite). Three sections of different orientation are usually required. Access to a good collection of anatomical preparations of modern and fossil woods is also essential for comparative purposes. Even with these aids in place, identification may only be possible to the family level. If preservation of cells is poor, identification may be impossible. It should also be noted that fragments of wood and bone can be very similar, and on casual inspection may be difficult to tell apart, even for an expert.

Fortunately, given moderate preservation, a good hand lens, and a cut or flattened transverse surface to work with, it is usually possible to place fossil

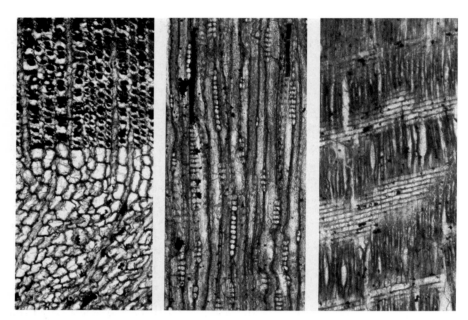

above: Composite photomicrograph showing transverse (left), tangential (centre) and radial (right) sections through fossil wood; *Cupressinoxylon* from the London Clay at Ashford, Kent, England (Eocene). Cells are approximately 30 μm in diameter.

wood within one of several broad categories. The most common types of wood encountered in the fossil record are angiosperms (flowering plants) and gymnosperms (conifers and relatives). Palms can be separated from other angiosperms by the presence of numerous vascular strands, which give the trunks a characteristic speckled appearance to the naked eye. Secondary wood is completely absent. Most angiosperms can be separated from gymnosperms on the presence of two cell types of distinctively different size. A good 8x magnifying glass is required to observe this feature. In angiosperm wood there is a sharp distinction between large cells called vessels and the more abundant smaller diameter fibre cells. In gymnosperms, all cells are basically of one type, and they are generally small. Angiosperm wood starts to become common in the middle part of the Cretaceous (about 120 million years ago), whereas wood with

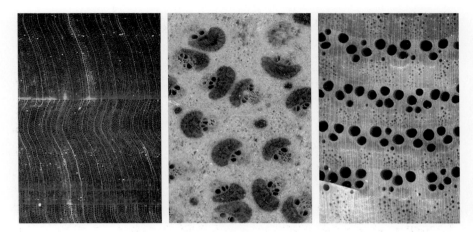

above: Composite photomicrograph comparing structures visible through a hand-held lens in transverse section of fossil tree trunks: gymnosperm (left), palm (centre) and angiosperm (right).

gymnospermous features has a much longer fossil record, extending back into the Late Palaeozoic (about 370 million years ago).

Fossil forests are no longer as puzzling as they once seemed. Much is known about the conditions under which they form, and nowadays we are able to understand their origin and evolution in the broader context of Earth history. No matter how enduring living forests appear to be when measured in human life spans, they are the products of a dynamic environment, albeit one in which changes occur imperceptibly slowly. On a geological timescale, forest composition and distribution has altered significantly. The driving forces are major shifts in Earth climate, the movement of continents, and the evolution of new plants and animals. For over 300 million years, forests have also been faithful recorders of environmental change. Reading these messages written in stone requires knowledge of the biology and ecology of living plants as well as a thorough investigation of the fossil record. Subsequent chapters will explore further some of these connections, focusing on the history of vegetation through time and touching on the origins of flowering plants in the final chapter. We turn next to the very special area of fossil plants as an energy resource.

Chapter Four

COAL
· · · · · · · ·

LAND-DWELLING PLANTS are among the most abundant and durable organisms in the fossil record. Those features that combine to enable plants to live and to thrive on land – such as the possession of cells with robust, resilient walls, and the presence of of resistant chemicals located in wood, bark and epidermis – also render them remarkably impervious to the ravages of time and to the rigours of rock formation. In most land environments, plants contribute by far the largest fraction of the world's biological matter. As they die or shed parts such as leaves, seeds and spores, a vast quantity botanical bits and pieces is dispersed and incorporated into soils and sediments of one sort or another. Over lengthy periods of geological time these remains can be converted into the insoluble carbon-rich residues that form the basis of fossil fuels. One of the most important of these is coal, which is a source of solar energy stored by plants during eons past.

Coal is a ubiquitous fuel, and major deposits have been discovered on every continent and in rocks of many different geological ages. It is little wonder then that this useful source of energy has been exploited by humans since Neolithic times. Our modern knowledge of coal stems from the industrial revolution that swept Europe during the nineteenth century. New machine driven industries needed a ready and cheap source of power. Coal provided the answer, and in doing so it became an exceptionally important

left: Brown coal (lignite) from the Mackenzie River, Canada (Eocene).

commodity; so much so that it is sometimes called 'black diamond'. In 1998, world production was estimated at 3.7 billion tonnes. This represents over a quarter of the world's primary energy needs, a figure that is exceeded only by oil. Coal currently provides 36 per cent of the world's electricity, and it is an essential ingredient in the manufacture of steel and iron, important building blocks of our modern world. Coal is much more than just a fossil fuel, it is an essential natural resource that impacts our everyday lives.

ANIMAL, VEGETABLE OR MINERAL?

At the turn of the eighteenth century, scientific discussion on the origin and formation of coal was a controversial business. Black coals are rather amorphous substances, and there have been several theories on how they might form. Richard Kirwan, a famous Irish chemist, thought that coal was a mineral deposit and that it was not of organic origin. His protagonist, James

above: Coal is formed from fossil plants. The regular pattern on the surface of this 14 cm-long piece is the impression of the bark of a fossil tree; *Lepidodendron* (Late Carboniferous, Coseley near Dudley, West Midlands, England).

Parkinson, an English naturalist, took another view. Parkinson argued that coal was demonstrably of vegetable origin because it was closely associated with fossil plants. The botanical origins of coal received further support when it was demonstrated that black coals were part of a continuous series going from obviously planty peat, through woody lignite (brown coal), bituminous coal, to amorphous anthracite. Further evidence was adduced by the extraction of microscopic spores from coal in the mid-1800s, and later by microscopic examination of coal in thin section. Two main types of coal are recognised today. The most common is humic coal, which is formed from land plants living in wetland environments such as swamps and bogs. Sapropelic coal (e.g. boghead coal) is formed mainly from algae living in oxygen-poor lakes.

Two additional properties of coal have important industrial and environmental consequences. The grade of a coal refers to properties such as its ash and sulphur content. Burning high sulphur coals leads to the production of sulphur dioxide gas, which is a major contributing factor to acid rain. The ash content of a coal refers to the material left over after burning. High ash coals have lower economic value, and they have the added disadvantage of producing a solid waste. Low ash and low sulphur content are therefore desirable qualities in coals. The rank of a coal is a measure of the level of alteration of peat to form coal. Rank increases through a series from peat, through lignite, sub-bituminous coal, bituminous coal, to anthracite. These changes are brought about by increases in temperature and pressure over geological time. Higher rank coals combine lower moisture and volatile matter content with a higher concentration of carbon and increased calorific value. These are generally desirable properties. The higher concentration of carbon in bituminous coals is useful in the production of coke, which is of importance in industries such as steel manufacture. Also, a higher calorific value gives more energy per unit weight of coal.

COAL FORMATION

Coal usually forms in areas of high rainfall and under waterlogged soil conditions. When soils are saturated with water, much of the oxygen needed for bacteria to decay plant tissues is excluded. This can lead to the accumulation of substantial depths of organic debris. Such environments are termed mires, and where soils contain more than 50 per cent organic matter they are termed peat. The accumulation of organic debris in this way is the first stage in the formation of coal.

RAINS AND FLOODS

The source of the water in mire formation is of major significance to the quality of the coal that will eventually be produced. The principal sources of water are either rainfall or through-flow from outside the mire. Water flowing through the system may be charged with nutrients and minerals. In particular, clay particles carried in will reduce the grade of the coal by increasing its ash content. Also, if incoming water is brackish rather than fresh it will have a high content of sulphate. This can lead to the formation of the iron sulphide mineral pyrite within the peat, ultimately reducing the grade of the coal by increasing its sulphur content. Peat that forms in mires fed mainly by rainfall is generally nutrient and clay poor, meaning that coals formed from this source are of higher grade. These types of peat can also grow to great thickness, giving rise to thick seams of coal. Coals formed in this way are generally of great economic value.

TIME AND PRESSURE

As peat accumulates, the action of bacteria on plant debris in the surface layers causes partial breakdown of plant tissues, releasing carbon dioxide, methane and water. Some of the by-products of decay react to produce yellow-brown humic acids, which further limit bacterial action. As more peat accumulates, pressure and temperature increase and bacterium-mediated decay gives way to geochemical processes. The outcome is further degradation of the original cellular structure and biochemical constituents of the plant material. More water and volatiles are lost leading to an increase in the carbon content. The density of the coal also increases with compaction. The degree of alteration from the original structure is a function of the temperature and pressure, which determines the rank of the coal. Geologically older coals tend to be of higher rank and so may be more valuable. Tertiary coals tend to be lignite or sub-bituminous, Mesozoic coals are sub-bituminous and bituminous, and Palaeozoic coals are usually bituminous or anthracites.

CYCLICAL PATTERNS

Studies of coal-bearing sequences frequently reveal a cyclical pattern of coal seams sandwiched between bands of sandstone or shales. This reflects changing environmental conditions on a local scale where the formation of peat has been interrupted by episodic flooding that deposited sand, silt and clay. Such patterns of cyclic or rhythmic sedimentation are called cyclothems. When we compare the thickness of the cyclothems seen in coal-bearing sequences from the geological record to modern analogues from the Everglades and Okefenokee swamps of the USA we learn some surprising facts. It takes over 10 m of peat to form 1 m of bituminous coal. This 10 m of peat can take over 7000 years to accumulate. However, it takes only 2–3 m of mud and silts to make 1 m of mudstones and siltstones. This 2–3 m of sediment can form in as little as five years. When an average coal cyclothem is examined, it has been calculated that floods occurred for only 2 per cent of the time, even though they account for 80–90 per cent of the thickness of the sedimentary sequence. Coal seams therefore represent very lengthy periods of stable environmental conditions during which coal swamp vegetation flourished.

CARBONIFEROUS – THE AGE OF COAL

Although coals have been reported in rocks from the Early Palaeozoic, the first major deposits were laid down during the upper part of the Carboniferous, between 295 and 320 million years ago. It is the coal that gives its name to the Carboniferous (Latin *carbo*, meaning coal; *ferre*, meaning to bear) and these coal-bearing sequences also go by the informal term of coal measures.

From a geographic perspective, the world of the Late Carboniferous was very different from today. Plate tectonic theory indicates that all of the

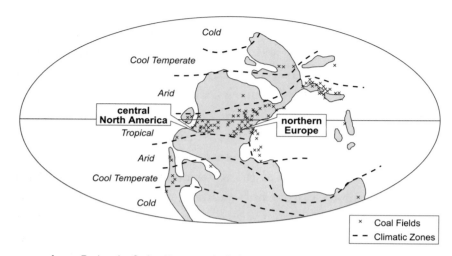

above: During the Carboniferous, a single large landmass called Pangea spanned the Northern and Southern Hemispheres. The greatest concentration of coal formed within the tropical belt.

continents were joined together in one landmass, called Pangea. This newly formed supercontinent stretched from the South Pole almost to the North Pole. One of the final acts in the formation of Pangea was the closure of the Rheic Ocean, an extinct tract of sea separating the northern landmasses of Laurasia (present day North America and Europe) from the southern landmass of Gondwana (present day South America, Africa, India, Australasia and Antarctica). The slow collision of these landmasses caused the crust to buckle creating broad lowlands fringed by a mountain chain that stretched across the tropics. It is in this setting of tropical lowlands bordering the closing Rheic Ocean that the first great coalfields of Asia, Europe and North America were formed.

Despite major differences in the configuration of the continents, the climate of the Late Carboniferous is thought to have been more similar to modern climates than any other period in Earth history. One reason for this is the existence of ice caps in the polar regions, which created a steep climatic gradient from pole to equator. This is a comparatively rare occurrence during the Phanerozoic and a feature that the Carboniferous shares with the world of today. This means that even though the climate of the coal forming equatorial region was tropical and wet, mid latitudes were cooler and more variable with wet and dry seasons, and at high latitudes cold temperate and arctic conditions prevailed.

Occasionally, within the Carboniferous coal bearing strata, there are thin layers of marine rocks. These are physical evidence of the episodic development of shallow epicontinental seas between periods of coal formation. One possible explanation for the intercalation of marine sequences is related to environmental change. Just like the recent ice age of the Pleistocene, the climate of the Carboniferous experienced the waxing and waning of ice sheets. It is likely that climatic fluctuations created distinct glacial and interglacial periods. These changes would have been accompanied by rising sea levels due to glacial melt. A sea level rise of only a few metres would have been enough to flood the Carboniferous lowlands bordering the southern coastal margin of Laurasia. As the climate returned to colder glacial conditions, more water would have been locked away in the ice caps and the sea level would have fallen again. Coal swamp environments were therefore particularly vulnerable to changes in sea level as well as to changing patterns of land drainage.

PLANTS OF THE COAL MEASURE FORESTS

The forests of the Late Carboniferous coal forming swamps have been likened to modern tropical rainforest, but this analogy is misleading in several respects. The comparison is based on the inference that both rainforest and coal swamp formed in areas of high rainfall and that they are particularly common in the humid tropics. But here the similarities end. In today's world, rainforest is dominated by flowering plants, many of which are long-lived woody trees. Over 10 per cent of the plant species are epiphytic, including abundant mosses and lichens. In contrast, flowers were completely absent form the Carboniferous coal swamps. A broader range of different plant groups coexisted than in today's forests, and they differed widely from each other in both body plan and reproductive biology. Many of the tree species were

above: Diorama of Carboniferous coal swamp displayed in Chicago's Field Museum.

probably short-lived and very rapidly growing. There is scant evidence for epiphytes, very little is known about the existence of true mosses and lichens, and although insects were abundant, vertebrate herbivores were non-existent. In short, despite a similar climatic regime, coal swamp forests have no close modern analogues.

LYCOPSIDS (CLUBMOSSES)

By far the largest plants were the lycopsids or clubmosses. Some species regularly attained a height of 30 m and a diameter of over 1 m at the base, and there is evidence to suggest that some grew to as much as 50 m in height. The most famous of these – and one of the most studied of all Carboniferous plants – is *Lepidodendron*. Mature specimens had a long straight trunk topped by a crown of bifurcating branches bearing simple leaves in a helical arrangement. The leaves had fleshy bases, which impart the characteristic diamond-shapes pattern to the bark. The leaves themselves were long and narrow like blades of grass. Unlike modern flowering plants and conifers, *Lepidodendron* reproduced by means of spores not seeds. These developed in cones that were borne at the ends of branches. At the other end of the trunk, the rooting system mirrored to a notable degree the structure of the crown. The main root comprised enormous bifurcating branches that bore simple rootlets in a helical arrangement. These spread out at right angles from the base of the trunk to form a much branched but rather shallow rooting platform. *Lepidodendron* and its kin inhabited the wettest parts of the coal swamps.

The habit and development of *Lepidodendron* trees was very different to the trees of today, and this had important consequences for their ecology. *Lepidodendron* has been likened to a giant herb. Unlike the trunks of flowering plants or conifers it produced very little wood. Most of the structural support came from a thick bark-like region. It has been estimated that the growth of these giant clubmosses would have been rapid and their entire lifespan may have lasted a mere 10–15 years. Also, growth was determinate. This means that many species produced their crown of branches in the final phase of life, an aspect that had consequences for the way that they reproduced. Because the crown of branches came last, and the spore-producing cones were borne at the tips of branches, it is likely that some species of *Lepidodendron* were monocarpic. In other words, some species reproduced only once towards the end of their

left: One concept of the extinct tree clubmoss *Lepidodendron,* which grew in excess of 30 m.

above: The reptilian appearance of the branch of this fossil tree is caused by the diamond-shaped pattern, which indicates the points of attachment of the leaves. This branch is approximately 6 cm in diameter. In the nineteenth century, trunks of *Lepidodendron* were exhibited at fairgrounds as giant fossil lizards or snakes.

life in one spectacular and massive outburst of spores.

The leafy canopy of Carboniferous swamp forest also differed in important ways from the dense closed canopy of modern rainforest. From examining preserved stands of trunks such as those at Victoria Park in Glasgow, Scotland (Chapter 3), it is surprising to learn that tree lycopsids grew at a greater density than is typical of trees in modern rainforest. It has been estimated that there could have been as many as 1000 to 2000 giant clubmosses per hectare. This density was possible because the trunk of *Lepidodendron* did not branch until nearly fully grown, so the plant spent most of its life as an unbranched pole. Also, the trunk bore long, thin, grass-like leaves, at least in its juvenile stages. The consequences of this growth form were that although the trees were closely spaced, light penetration to the forest floor would have been comparatively high. Forest floor dwelling plants would have had a better quality of light in the Carboniferous coal swamps than do their modern rainforest equivalents.

The tree lycopsids were an incredibly diverse group comprising three or more family level units. Most were large plants, but some lost the ability to produce a trunk and reverted to a sort of squat pseudo-herbaceous habit. The

above: Petrified cone of a tree clubmoss: entire cone (left); section across cone (right), approximately 5 cm in diameter, showing spore-containing sacs radiating out from a central point like the spokes of a wheel; *Flemingites* (*Lepidostrobus*) *brownii* (Carboniferous, France).
below: Leaves of tree clubmoss *Cyperites bicarinatus* (Late Carboniferous, Kilmersdon, near Radstock, Somerset, England). Block measures approximately 15 cm.

major groups differed in their form of branching, their type of reproduction, and whether or not they produced spores once or over an extended period of several years. They also had different ecological preferences. Some were colonisers of disturbed habitats, whereas others preferred to grow in more stable, well established soils. Although generally preferring very wet soil conditions, there is much evidence that variations in soil water and clay content were exploited

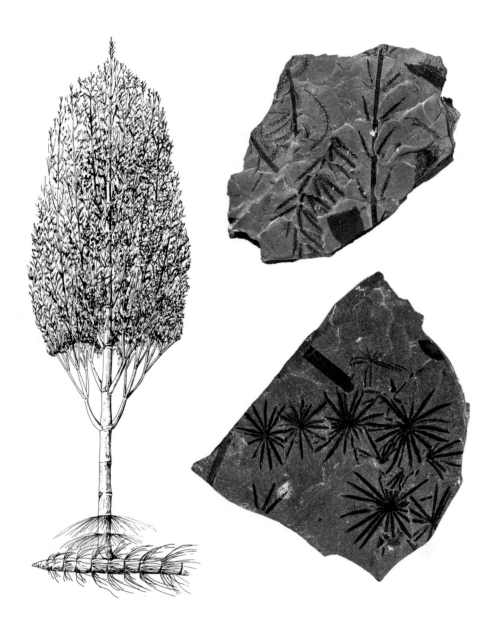

left: *Calamites*: a horsetail the size of a tree (approximately 10 m high).
top right: Branches of *Calamites* bearing leaves and cones; *Palaeostachya* and
Asterophyllites (Late Carboniferous, Wales). Block measures approximately 15 cm.
above right: The leaves of *Calamites* were borne in whorls, approximately
15 mm in size; *Annularia radiata* (Late Carboniferous, Wales).

by different species in different ways. It was these coal swamp giants that contributed much of the biomass to Carboniferous coals.

HORSETAILS AND THEIR RELATIVES

A second group of coal swamp trees is closely related to living horsetails (scouring rushes) in the genus *Equisetum*. Unlike its modern relatives, which are all small herbaceous plants, the extinct *Calamites* was a large woody tree that grew to about 10 m in height. Otherwise, there is no mistaking this plant because it strongly resembles living horsetails. The stems had a distinctive segmented appearance and vertical ribbing, superficially resembled a thick bamboo cane. All the parts, branches, leaves and cones, were borne in whorls. The leaves were needle shaped and up to 25 per whorl. Like the tree

clubmosses, *Calamites* reproduced by means of spores, and these were produced in small sacs organised into cones. This group of trees was a persistent minor component of Carboniferous mires, favouring disturbed environments such as streams and lake margins.

The stems of modern *Equisetum* are brittle and very lightweight. One reason for this is that they contain numerous elongated air-filled channels. These were also a feature of *Calamites*, and they were responsible for a particular mode of fossilisation of the stem. When a *Calamites* trunk toppled, the large central air-filled channel within the stem could rapidly become filled with sediment forming an inner cast. Following decay of the outer tissues only the internal mould remained, and it is this that is most frequently found in the fossil record. Another distinctive feature of living *Equisetum* is the extensive subterranean rhizome. It is this feature that enables the plant to develop extensive clones,

above: Natural cast of trunk interior of *Calamites*, approximately 40 cm in length. Curvature indicates that this specimen comes from near the base of the tree (Late Carboniferous).

above: Slender forest floor-dwelling or vining *Sphenophyllum* (Late Carboniferous, Wales). Block measures approximately 30 cm.

making some species successful and invasive weeds. Massive underground rhizomes were also a feature of extinct *Calamites*, which is the only group of trees with a clonal habit.

Not all of the horsetail relatives of the Carboniferous coal swamps were trees. One group, called the sphenophylls, were small herbaceous plants. Like horsetails, the leaves were borne in whorls along the stem, and the plant reproduced by spores that developed in cones borne on the ends of branches. The leaves are on the whole much broader than those of horsetails. The habit of *Sphenophyllum* has not been worked out in detail, but some species are thought to have been climbing vine-like plants.

FERNS

Coal swamp forests were home to a very broad assortment of ferns with a similar range of habits and ecologies to those of modern day rainforest. Tree ferns formed part of the canopy and they were particularly abundant in the latter part of the age of the coal swamps. Others were ground dwelling or scrambling, and some species are thought to have been epiphytes on the trunks of the larger tree ferns.

The most common ferns of the coal measure swamps were the tree ferns. These bore a superficial resemblance to the modern tree ferns *Dicksonia* and *Cyathea*, which are widely grown as ornamental garden plants. Carboniferous tree ferns belong to a different family called the Marattiales. One such plant from the Late Carboniferous was called *Psaronius*. This was a small tree about 8–10 m tall with fronds as long as 3 m. The fronds grew from the top of the trunk where they started life as tightly curled crosiers. In popular terms these

above left: Restoration of the extinct tree fern *Psaronius*, approximately 8-10 m in height (Late Carboniferous-Permian).
above right: Fern foliage (Late Carboniferous, Wales), block measures approximately 25 cm.

are called 'fiddle-heads'. The trunks of *Psaronius* – like those of tree ferns in general – grew in a completely different manner to the trunks of conifers and flowering plant trees. In the centre was a narrow cylinder of tissues that was formed mainly from the bases of leaves and the vascular tissues that feed these. Surrounding this and making up the bulk of the trunk was a mantle of roots. Individual roots developed from the growing point in the crown and grew downwards to ensheath the trunk. When stems of *Psaronius* were petrified in silica, they produced very attractive fossils with striking geometric patterns fashioned from the central cylinder and the root mantle.

Because of the way that they grow, the trunks of tree ferns are tough and lightweight. In modern rainforest, their fibrous texture makes them an ideal medium for other plants to root into, and they can support quite a diverse flora of epiphytes (e.g. orchids and bromeliads). There is evidence to suggest that during the Carboniferous, some species of ferns actually lived as epiphytes on tree trunks. One such fern is called *Botryopteris*. In this case evidence comes the observation of *Botryopteris* entwined in the root mantle of the petrified trunks of *Psaronius*.

SEED FERNS

Frequently in the fossil record one encounters extinct groups with novel combinations of characters. We have seen in Chapter 2 how the extinct tree *Archaeopteris* combined the leaves and reproductive organs of a fern with the woody trunk of a conifer; a combination of features not seen among any living species. The coal swamp forests harboured their own bizarre and interesting extinct groups. One of these was the seed ferns, also called pteridosperms. True ferns reproduce by producing microscopic spores, whereas seed ferns combined a fern-like frond with a mode of reproduction involving seeds. Much of the fern-like foliage of the coal swamp floras therefore does not belong to ferns

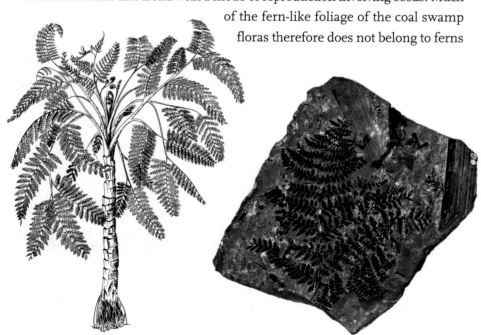

above: Despite the name and appearance, the seed fern *Medullosa noei* is not a true fern. It had a woody trunk, bore large seeds, and was approximately 3.5 m in height.

above: Fern-like foliage of early gymnosperm, *Neuropteris heterophylla*, approximately 40 cm long (Late Carboniferous, Derbyshire, England).

at all, but to an extinct group of plants that is actually more closely related to conifers and flowers. The seed ferns were woody plants that encompassed growth habits ranging from small trees to prostrate, scrambling or vining types. The fronds were fern-like, and the seeds were borne in groups on special branches and in various positions on the leaves. The trees belonged to the so-called medullosan pteridosperms, and these bore a superficial resemblance to true tree ferns. The trunks of medullosans were composed primarily of bundles of leaf bases. Unlike the true tree ferns however, these contained substantial amounts of wood and they were very rich in resins. The fronds, seeds and pollen grains of medullosans were on the whole very large. Fronds developed from the crown, and they grew to over 7 m in length. Seeds were borne along the midrib or at the margins of the fronds, and they could exceed 7 cm in size. At 0.3 mm in diameter, pollen grains were five to ten times larger than average, leading to the suggestion that the medullosans were pollinated by insects.

Medullosan pteridosperms were common throughout the Carboniferous. Their preference was for mineral rich rather than peaty substrates. They seem to have existed in fire-prone parts of the mire, and their resinous trunks and the large quantities of foliage may have been an important source of fuel for forest fires.

THE FIRST CONIFERS

Hidden among the giant and exotic, the coal swamp forests harboured plants that were close relatives of some modern trees and shrubs. The extinct group Cordaitales bore similarities to conifers. Cordaites were woody plants that came in a

above: Many early gymnosperms were shrubs. Reconstruction of *Cordaixylon*, which measured approximately 2 m in height.

above: Long strap-shaped leaf of early gymnosperm *Cordaites borassifolius*, approximately 40 cm long (Late Carboniferous, Cannelton, Pennsylvania, USA). **above right:** Foliage of early conifer *Walchia piniformis*, approximately 30 cm long (Permian, Ardoisiers de Lodeve, Montpellier, France).

variety of shapes and sizes, ranging from large trees as much as 30 m tall to robust-stemmed prostrate shrubs. Seeds and pollen were borne in cones clustered on modified branches. Whereas the wood, cones, pollen and seeds resemble conifers, the leaves of cordaites were rather different. Conifers, on the whole, have small scale-like or needle-like leaves. Those of cordaites were up to 1 m long and strap-shaped. They bore some resemblance to the leaves of the living conifer *Agathis* and to those of flowers in the daffodil family (Amaryllidaceae) such as *Hippeastrum* (*Amaryllis*). Cordaites inhabited swamps along marine shores and estuaries. Some scientists think that these trees had stilt-like roots, which would be consistent with a mangrove habitat.

At some distance from the coal swamps and on higher ground were plants that resemble still more closely modern conifers. One such group is the Voltziales. In habit and in the structure of the wood, these were quite different from cordaites to which they are closely related. Voltziales were large trees that bore pollen and seeds in cones at the tips of leafy branches. Like living conifers in the pine family (Pinaceae) they had needle-like leaves. In overall habit, Voltziales probably bore a strong resemblance to conifers in the Araucariaceae (Monkey-Puzzle family).

PUTTING THE PIECES TOGETHER

When plants are small, piecing together their fossilised remains is a relatively straightforward business, but as they become larger the chance of finding entire specimens diminishes. Large plants come in bits and pieces that have been scrambled and sorted during the fossilisation process. Putting the pieces back together is like reassembling a jigsaw puzzle. But, this is a jigsaw puzzle with a difference: half the pieces are missing and the picture on the front of the box has been thrown away. In fact, it is more difficult even than this. Imagine putting together in the correct order five or ten or more jigsaw puzzles that have been mixed up. One approach would be to begin by sorting the bits into groups and as more and more pieces are found to gradually reassemble the whole. Even with only half the picture, you may recognise what the whole will look like despite not having all of the details. This is the approach taken by palaeobotanists in reassembling fossil plants.

Because large plants often have to be reassembled from small pieces, various plant organs have been given their own unique names. In other words, the pieces of the jigsaw are 'tagged' and noted as they are found. In 1820, the bark of the giant tree clubmoss was given the name *Lepidodendron* long before the whole plant was known in any detail. Likewise, the rooting organs were called *Stigmaria*. Other organs have received various names depending on their state of preservation and the degree of confidence to which we can assign them to one of several related whole plant concepts. For example, leaves have been called *Lepidophylloides*, *Sigillariopsis*, and *Cyperites*, and leaves bearing spore sacs were called *Lepidostrobophyllum*. Similarly, the cones have received a variety of names, some of which are dependent on their state of preservation and others on whether they contain small spores or large spores. The spores too have their own names. As the organism became better understood and the various parts were linked together, the reconstructed whole plant became known as *Lepidodendron*. The development of this concept of root connected to trunk, branches and cones took many years to complete. Reconstructions of this sort generally do not represent individuals. They are better thought of as hypotheses or concepts of what the plant actually looked like, the accuracy of which depends upon the nature of the evidence used in their development.

COAL BALLS AND OTHER CONCRETIONS

Our knowledge of Carboniferous coal swamp floras is based on a rich mixture of fossil evidence ranging from plant bits visible to the naked eye, to microscopic evidence adduced from the waxy cuticles of leaves, to miniscule but extremely abundant and widespread spores. One particular type of fossil – the concretion – is particularly informative because of the detail it conveys on the internal structure of plants.

Concretions are widespread in Carboniferous rocks and they can form from several different types of mineral. One common type is the ironstone nodule. These egg-shaped or elongate nodules frequently contain animals or plant parts. The puzzle of how the fossil gets into the centre of these stones is solved by understanding the way that they form. Ironstone nodules are composed of the mineral siderite ($FeCO_3$), which can precipitate out of solution in response to very localised changes in pH caused by the proximity of decaying organisms. In this way, fragments of plant or animal become the nucleus for a volume of precipitating mineral, which eventually becomes cemented forming the nodule. The formation of ironstone nodules occurs in most of the world's Upper Carboniferous strata. Famous sites include Mazon Creek, Illinois, USA, and the Lancashire and West Midlands Coalfields, England.

Occasionally within bituminous coal bearing strata, mining operations are disrupted by large limestone concretions. Miners call these 'bastard limestone' because they are a nuisance, damaging shovelling and sorting equipment. To palaeobotanists, however, these concretions, known as coal balls, are highly prized because inside are the fossilised remains of plants preserved in three

above: The earliest seeds were small and borne in lobed structures called cupules; *Xenotheca devonica* (Late Devonian, Devon, England) (cupules about 10 mm long).

above: Living analogue: bryophytes such as *Anthoceros* have a similar level of structural complexity to the first land plants. The spore-bearing parts are green, stick-like and approximately 1 mm in diameter.

above: The Water Horsetail (*Equisetum fluviatile*): a handful of living species make up this ancient and once diverse group.

left: Massed stick-like stems of early land plants preserved in a fine-grained shale block, approximately 27 cm wide. *Thursophyton elberfeldense* (Early Devonian, Germany).

above: Echoes of the Devonian Explosion: the Stag's Horn Clubmoss, *Lycopodium clavatum*, closely resembles some early land plants (left); leaves of the Royal Fern, *Osmunda regalis* (right).

above: Conifers were the dominant forest tree throughout most of the Mesozoic. Modern *Araucaria araucana* forest in Nahuel Buta cordillera of Angol, Chile.

above: Volcanic terrain of Mount St Helens (pictured in background), following volcanic explosion and pyroclastic flow, showing felled trees in ash, north fork of Toutle River Valley, 1982.

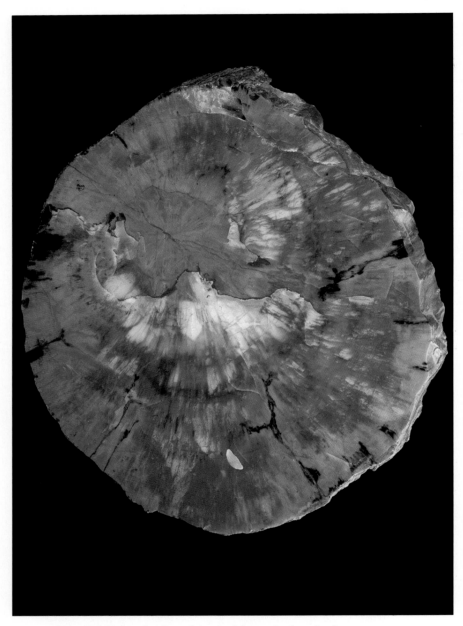

above: Polished section through trunk of *Araucarioxylon arizonicum*, the dominant conifer of Petrified Forest National Park, Arizona, USA, width approximately 25 cm (Late Triassic).

above: Polished section through trunk of *Quercus* (Oak), width approximately 33 cm, Saddle Mountain, Washington, USA (Miocene).

above: Petrified conifer trunk with precious opal, width approximately 10 cm, from White Cliffs, New South Wales, Australia (Late Cretaceous).
left: Polished section through trunk of the tree fern *Psaronius*, width approximately 15 cm, from Chemnitz, Germany (Permian).

above: Masses of minute disk-like spores provide evidence on the formation of this Russian coal (Carboniferous, Pobiedenko near Moscow, Russia).

above: Large nut-like seeds of *Trigonocarpus parkinsoni*, approximately 2.5 cm long, were produced by seed ferns (Late Carboniferous, Bolton, England).

above: Petrified tree fern trunk in cross section: the central stem is encased in a fibrous mantle of roots *Psaronius brasiliensis*, approximately 22 cm in diameter (Permian-Carboniferous, Rio Grande do Sul, Brazil).

above left: Fossil conifer cone, approximately 1.5 cm wide, collected in 1851 by Robert McClure whilst shipwrecked on Banks Island in the Canadian Arctic, *c.* 73°N (Miocene). Fossils such as this provide evidence of lush forests in the remote geological past where today there is only sparse tundra vegetation.
above right: Palm frond from Aix en Provence, France (Eocene). Block is approximately 32 cm long.

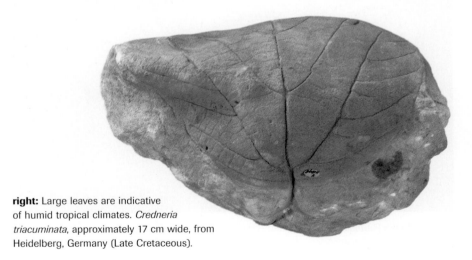

right: Large leaves are indicative of humid tropical climates. *Credneria triacuminata*, approximately 17 cm wide, from Heidelberg, Germany (Late Cretaceous).

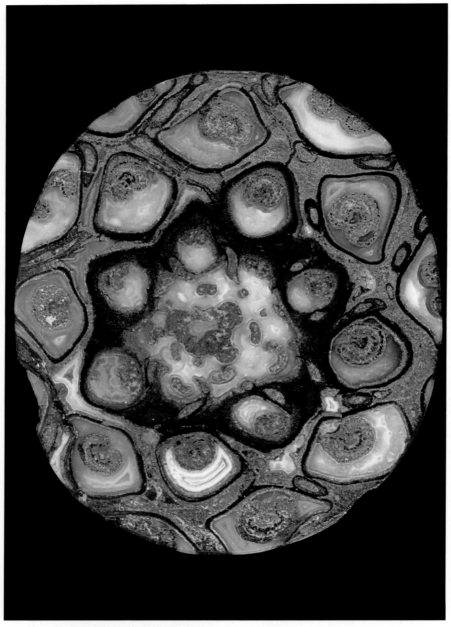

above: Petrified trunk of the fern *Palaeosmunda williamsonii*, approximately 4 cm wide, from Rockhampton, Queensland, Australia (Permian).

left: Extinct relative of the living Maidenhair Tree. Leaves of *Ginkgo huttonii* from the Jurassic of Scalby Ness, Yorkshire, England. Block is approximately 18 cm long.
below: Common plants of the Palaeophytic. Part of a petrified trunk of the tree fern *Tubicaulis africanus*, approximately 14 cm wide, from the Permian of Tanganyika, Africa.

above: Gondwanan fern. Foliage of *Cladophlebis australis* from Beaudesert, Queensland, Australia (Jurassic). Block approximately 7 cm long.

above: The discovery of a new coniferous tree 200 km north-east of Sydney, Australia in 1994 was a botanical sensation. Foliage of the so-called Wollemi Pine is similar to fossils such as *Agathis australis* from the Jurassic of Talbragar, New South Wales, Australia. Leaf is approximately 15 cm long.

above: Towards the end of the Triassic, foliage of *Glossopteris* gave way to *Dicroidium* in Gondwana. Leaf of *Dicroidium superbum*, approximately 25 cm long, from the Triassic of Brookvale, New South Wales, Australia.

above: Tongue-shaped leaves of *Glossopteris* are characteristic of the Permian and Triassic rocks of Gondwana. Leaves of *Glossopteris browniana*, approximately 35 cm long, from the Permian of Nagpur, India.

above: Peas in a pod: the variety of fruits increased from the Late Cretaceous through to the Paleocene. *Prosopis linearifolia* pod, approximately 6.5 cm long, from the Late Eocene of Florissant, Colorado, USA.

above: Eaten alive: a thin dark edge to this bite mark is evidence that the leaf was living when it was nibbled (from the Middle Eocene of Bournemouth, England). Living plants can form scar tissues in response to insect damage.

above: Early flowers were small and on the whole simple with little differentiation of sepals and petals, and in many the anthers released pollen through flap-like valves as in the modern avocado pear (*Persea americana*: Lauraceae).

below: Insect pollinator: female sphecid wasp preserved in Burmese amber. New research indicates that these deposits are of mid-Cretaceous age (about 100 million years old). *Cretospilomena familiaris* from the Hukawng Valley region of Myanmar.

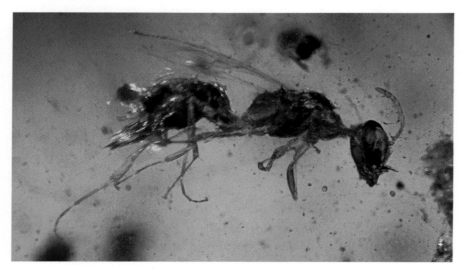

above: Egg-shaped or sausage-shaped ironstone nodules containing fossil plants are common at some Carboniferous sites; *Paripteris pseudogigantea*, approximately 16 cm long (Late Carboniferous, Coseley near Dudley, West Midlands, England).

dimensions and with cellular structures intact. In coal balls, the plant cells become filled with a crystalline form of calcium carbonate that brings a halt to further decay, provides internal support for the cell walls, and is resistant to compaction during burial in sediment. It is for these reasons that coal balls are a true palaeobotanical treasure trove.

Palaeobotanists discovered the remarkable ability of coal balls to preserve the cell structure of plants as far back as the 1850s. Nowadays, coal balls are investigated using the peel technique. The principle of this technique is to reconstruct the external form and the internal structure of plants by serial sections. The coal ball is first cut with a diamond saw. The cut surface is ground smooth using abrasives and then briefly etched by immersion in weak hydrochloric acid. This acid dissolves away some of the mineral encasing and

above left: Cannon-ball sized or larger, more or less spherical calcium carbonate concretions are common at many Carboniferous sites. These so-called coal balls (specimen 8 cm in diameter) contain the exquisitely preserved petrified remains of fossil plants (Late Carboniferous, England).
above right: Tissues of petrified plants preserved in cut coal ball.

infilling the plant tissues, leaving the coalified cell walls slightly proud of the surface. The next stage is to transfer these organic remains to an acetate sheet. This is achieved by flooding the etched surface of the coal ball in the solvent acetone (nail varnish remover). Before this has time to evaporate, a thin, transparent acetate sheet (e.g. an overhead projector transparency sheet) is laid gently onto the etched coal ball surface. The cell walls bond to the acetate sheet, which can be peeled away, and the process is repeated to make serial sections. The 'peel' can then be stored for later analysis or examined to reveal the cellular details of the plants.

There are several theories on how coal balls form. Most scientists agree that the process involves water rich in dissolved minerals percolating through the peat during the coal and rock forming process (diagenesis). They also agree that this process can occur very early in the deposition of the peat, so early in fact that the creation of the coal ball can actually be the cause of death for the plants it preserves. It is in this type of coal ball that the most exceptional preservation occurs. Coal balls can also form at a later stage after some compaction and decay has occurred to the plant tissues.

Scientists have yet to find the definitive answer to the formation of coal balls. It is the source of the dissolved carbonate and the factors causing its precipitation on a local scale that are the main areas of controversy. Sea water is one potential source of carbonate. Occasional marine incursions could have introduced calcium and magnesium carbonates in a dissolved form into the coal swamp peat. Another possibility is that marine muds were ripped up and deposited in coal swamps during storm induced flooding. This is consistent with the occasional discovery of marine animals within coal balls. A third possibility is that the carbonate comes from groundwater percolating upwards through the swamp. This is consistent with some geochemical evidence from oxygen and carbon isotopes. Any one of these hypotheses might be correct, and it is possible that all three sources could have produced coal balls in the same sequence of rocks at different times.

Hundreds of thousands of hours of research over a period of nearly 200 years have unlocked the secrets of coal, revealing much about its formation and at the same time bringing to life the very ancient and mysterious environments of the coal swamp forests. The giant clubmosses and horsetails have long since disappeared, but thanks to a very particular set of geological and environmental circumstances it is still possible to learn a great deal about the biology of these unfamiliar plants and to investigate the ecology of the swamps in which they grew. We can peer back into the Carboniferous and observe plant life on land with a clarity that is seldom matched in other geological periods. We have touched on some examples here, which barely do justice to the enormous mine of information that we now possess on coal swamp forests. These swamps were the nurseries of many major groups of living plants, and many pieces of the jigsaw still need to be found or placed in context. The economic importance of coal has diminished somewhat with the rise of oil and gas. But, the Sun that shone down from a tropical sky 300 million years ago burns brightly today through the power of coal, which still provides much heat and light for our electronic world.

Chapter Five

MEASURING THE PAST
· ·

THE SOLID BOUNDARIES of geography and the stable pattern of climatic zones that form such important frames of reference in today's world are comforting illusions that dissolve into a confusingly dynamic picture over geological time. Ever since the early part of the seventeenth century it has been known that the Earth has experienced sweeping changes in climate over vast stretches of time. The earliest evidence came from the fossilised remains of animals and plants. As naturalists began to unearth examples of fossilised shells and corals in rocks of high latitude temperate regions, they noted that in many instances these were closely related to modern species living in the tropics. This curious pattern was repeated with other temperature-sensitive groups, such as reptiles and turtles. More remarkable still were the discoveries made in rocks of the Arctic regions. Early nineteenth-century explorers brought back fossil plants from Arctic Canada and the islands off the northern coasts of Scandinavia and Russia. These finds were to yield direct evidence of lush vegetation in areas of the world where nowadays climates are too cold and dry and the winters are too long and dark to support a comparable flora. The inescapable conclusion reached by the mid-1800s was that climates of northern Europe and North America must have been very different in the past. Underpinning

left: Growth rings in the branch of a fossil conifer tell a tale of seasonal climates during the Cretaceous Period. *Cupressinoxylon luccombense*, approximately 3 cm in diameter (Luccomb Chine, Isle of Wight, England).

our knowledge of climate change is a detailed understanding of the biology of living plants and the distribution and classification of fossils.

FOSSILS AS THERMOMETERS

The potential of using fossils to gauge parameters of past climates, such as temperature and humidity, was realised long ago. In the 1830s, Charles Lyell articulated several of the underlying principles in his three-volume magnum opus *Principles of Geology*. These ideas were followed up by the Swiss Palaeobotanist Oswald Heer, who was the first to make a detailed systematic study of Arctic floras. In 1860, Heer published a landmark book on the climate history of the Tertiary in which he drew on evidence from fossil plants to make inferences about climate and temperature in the past. The basic principles advocated by Lyell and Heer are still applied today.

NEAREST LIVING RELATIVE

One approach to using fossil plants to investigate climate change makes use of classifications and our knowledge of the environmental tolerances of living species. This is called the 'nearest living relative' approach. If we find a fossil that can be classified within a modern group that is today only found in humid tropical climates then it is reasonable to draw the inference that the fossil had similar climatic tolerances. The foliage and fruits of palms are widespread in rocks of northern Europe in the Eocene 55–34 million years ago. Some of the largest fruits resemble those of the modern *Nypa* palm, which today is characteristic of forests of tropical south east Asia, where it grows in association with other types of mangrove vegetation. A comparison with modern relatives therefore implies the existence of a tropical climate as well as a mangrove environment in parts of northern Europe during the Eocene.

The reading of climatic signals from fossil plants based on the nearest living relative approach is a conceptually simple idea, but it is not without problems. Identification and recognition of close modern relatives are obviously key issues. The further that one goes back in time, the more difficult it is to identify close kin. Also, one of the underlying assumptions is that the climatic tolerances of a plant group remain unchanged through time. But, how can we be sure that this is so? Maybe the *Nypa*-like palms of the Eocene tolerated a broader range of climatic regimes than do their modern counterparts. If this were the case, then our knowledge of the ecological preferences of the modern species would be misleading. The answer to this problem lies in repeated observations of a similar nature across many different groups of plants and animals. As we begin to uncover and describe more fossils, so it becomes possible to assign many of them to modern groups of known temperature requirements and

above: Fossilised fruits resembling those of the modern *Nypa* palm can reach the size of a coconut. *Nipadites burtini*, approximately 13 cm long (Eocene, Schaerbeek, near Brussels, Belgium).

ecological preferences. It is therefore possible to build up multiple independent lines of evidence that attest to a particular climatic regime.

GROWTH RINGS

Another approach to drawing inferences about climate from fossil plants makes use of functional rather than taxonomic comparisons. Here, one is simply looking at aspects of the shape and form of a plant that are known to be linked to environmental variables. One of the most obvious examples of this is the presence of growth rings in wood. These are the product of seasonal variation in the activity of a layer of cells called the cambium at the bark/wood interface. This layer adds to both wood and bark, increasing the girth of a tree. Cessation of cell division may occur during winter or during periods of excessive aridity, leading to the formation of rings. The ring boundaries are formed by the contrast between the large cells produced at the beginning of the growing season (earlywood) and the smaller cells produced towards the end of the previous growing season (latewood). Because growth rings are usually formed on an annual basis, the approximate age of a temperate forest tree can be calculated by counting the rings in the lower part of the trunk. Rings are absent or less distinct under climatic regimes where vigorous growth can be sustained year round, such as in some tropical environments. The presence of rings in fossil wood can therefore be indicative of seasonality.

Growth ring analysis in wood was pioneered by the American scientist Andrew E Douglass in the early 1900s. It is said that Douglass began his research in 1904 by acquiring sections of wood from his local sawmill in Flagstaff, Arizona. On careful examination of the microscopic structure he noted a pattern in the rings. In particular, there was a distinct group of narrower rings at 21 rings in from the bark. Later that year, while examining an old tree stump on a rancher's farm he observed a similar pattern of rings, but here there was a total of 11 rather than 21 between the bark and the distinctive inner group of narrower rings. Using this information, Douglass astonished the owner of the ranch by correctly deducing that his tree had been felled in the year 1894. This principle is used in the science of dendrochronology, enabling wood fragments of unknown age to be dated with reference to a calibrated set of tree rings. Chronologies based on bristlecone pines (*Pinus aristata*) from the White Mountains of California, USA, go back almost 9000 years. Thus tree rings can be used to establish the year in which an event took place in the recent past.

The distinctive patterns of narrow and broad rings that enabled Douglass to link two pieces of wood from different trees are a measure of the conditions under which trees grow throughout their lifespan. Wood is therefore a kind of natural recording device that can transmit information on the environment, providing one knows how to read it. The year-to-year variations in ring width can be read as a story of how growing conditions for a tree have varied on an annual basis. In temperate ecosystems the ratio of earlywood to latewood is indicative of the length of the growing season. A higher ratio of latewood indicates a longer and more favourable episode of growth. However, this correlation may not hold in the tropics. Furthermore, fossils show that latewood was limited in trees that grew in polar regions. In these unfamiliar environments, light periodicity might have been the principal influence on ring structure rather than water and temperature. One must therefore look carefully at other environmental indications when interpreting the evidence from fossil wood.

Measurements of other aspects of ring structure can provide clues on environmental conditions within a single season of growth. For example, a late frost might cause actual physical damage or at least temporary cessation of cell division, which produces a feature that is termed a frost ring. A 'false ring' may be caused by a severe drought in the growing season. This will result in the production of very few small cells which mimic the end of season boundary within the ring. Drought rings usually exhibit a diminution of cell size, cell wall thickening or both. Careful observation can usually distinguish them from annual rings. However, if drought happens very late in the season this can be more difficult to detect.

above: False rings in fossil wood document interruptions in growth brought about by environmental perturbations during the growing season. *Cupressinoxylon luccombense* (Cretaceous, Luccomb Chine, Isle of Wight, England). Field of view is approximately 10 mm.

LEAF MARGINS

While Douglass was developing his tree ring methods, two other American scientists IW Bailey and EW Sinnott published a paper in 1915 that demonstrated a correlation between the shapes of leaves and various environmental parameters, such as temperature and water availability. Based on an analysis of flowering trees and shrubs from various regions, Bailey and Sinnott observed that the higher the proportion of species bearing leaves with toothed margins, the cooler the climate. They also noted that very cold or cold and dry climates have higher than expected proportions of smooth-edged leaves, bucking this general trend. Bearing this caveat in mind, these observations were interesting because they immediately suggested an additional way of obtaining information about climates of the past. The leaves of flowering plants are common fossils in the Cenozoic, so Bailey and Sinnott suggested that observations of the margins of fossilised leaves could provide a kind of botanical index to mean annual temperatures at the time the fossils formed.

above: Leaves with toothed margins are more common in temperate climates.
Populus attenuata, approximately 6 cm wide (Miocene, Oeningen, near Baden, Germany).

If the nature of the leaf margin affords a kind of palaeontological thermometer, then what about other characteristics of leaves and other climate variables? Extreme modern environments provide case studies of how the leaves of plants have evolved to meet the challenges imposed by climate. In deserts plants must minimise water loss, so the leaves of shrubs and other perennials are small. In some extreme forms, such as cacti, the function of photosynthesis has been transferred to the stem, and the leaves serve only as a thorny barrier to fend off would be grazers. On the other hand, in tropical rainforests plants do not need to invest so heavily in making the most of water because it is more readily available. Leaf surface area does not need to be so constrained, so it can be expanded to furnish a more efficient platform for intercepting light. Tropical rainforests are home to plants with some of the largest leaves of all. Rainfall in the tropics can be so persistent that leaves have special margins to cope with this. Many tropical species bear leaves with a so-called 'drip tip', which is a kind of pointed end that facilitates water runoff. So, in addition to providing clues about temperature, certain aspects of leaf form can be used to gauge patterns of rainfall.

Jack A Wolfe at the University of Arizona extended Bailey and Sinnott's methodology to consider how a range of other leaf characteristics such as size, shape, and other aspects of the leaf margin, correlate with environmental parameters such as annual rainfall, annual temperature and elevation. Working with living species from a broad range of environments, Wolfe and colleagues developed an extensive database of measurements taken from the leaves of plants growing close to meteorological stations. In this way they were able to relate leaf parameters to an accurate record of climatic variables over extended periods. Using multivariate statistics, they compared leaf characteristics and environmental parameters. Measurements taken from the leaves of fossil floras can be compared directly to this database, thereby providing estimates of temperature and rainfall. This method has been dubbed CLAMP analysis, and the acronym stands for Climate Leaf Analysis Multivariate Programme. CLAMP analysis, as currently developed, is applicable to floras containing flowering plant leaf fossils in sediments of Late Cretaceous and Cenozoic age.

THE CARBON DIOXIDE BAROMETER

The study of climate change over short historical timescales has shown that Earth has warmed significantly over the last 140 years. Global warming on this scale is widely acknowledged, but its causes are debated. Some scientists attribute much of the recent change to natural causes, such as the number and size of volcanic eruptions or fluctuations in solar activity, whereas others emphasise the effects of human activities, in particular the burning of fossil fuels. It is known that certain constituents of the atmosphere, in particular water vapour and carbon dioxide gas, have an important role to play in regulating Earth's surface temperature. These and other gases are thought to drive the so-called 'greenhouse effect', which has played a major role in the debate on global warming.

The greenhouse effect works by trapping solar energy near the Earth's surface in much the same way that a botanical glasshouse warms the air within. Light from the Sun (short wave radiation) passes through the atmosphere heating the surface of the Earth. As objects on the surface heat up they emit greater amounts of thermal radiation (long wave radiation), which passes back through the atmosphere and out into space. Some of this

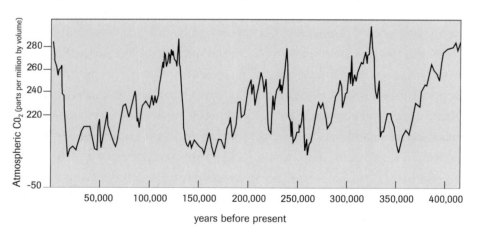

above: The ups and downs of carbon dioxide in the atmosphere over the past 420,000 years as measured from ice cored from the Antarctic. The five main peaks correspond to interglacial periods and the long deeper troughs are where glacial conditions prevailed.

thermal radiation is absorbed by gasses such as carbon dioxide and water vapour, slowing down the release of heat into space. This is why clear nights tend to be cooler than cloudy ones. The greater the amount of water vapour or carbon dioxide in the atmosphere, the greater the retention effect. Since the concentration of carbon dioxide gas has increased by more than 20

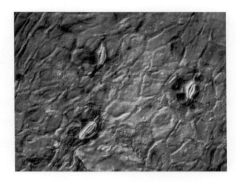

above: Microscopic stomata in fossil leaves, *Gingko huttoni* (Jurassic, Yorkshire, England).

per cent over the last 200 years, some scientists attribute recent global warming to this effect, which is a consequence of burning fossil fuels. Others argue that higher levels of atmospheric carbon dioxide are a symptom rather than a cause of global warming. In either event, higher levels of atmospheric carbon dioxide seems to correlate with higher global temperatures, and evidence from Antarctic ice cores shows that this relationship holds for the previous 400,000 years. So if we could measure the levels of this gas in the atmosphere further back in time, we would have another proxy measure of temperature fluctuation through time.

One approach to measuring fluctuations in the concentration of atmospheric carbon dioxide uses an intriguing idea developed by the British scientist FI Woodward. It has long been known that plants take up carbon dioxide from the atmosphere through microscopic pores in the epidermis called stomata, and that these can be preserved in the cuticles of fossilised leaves. Experiments have also shown that in some species the density of these stomata varies depending upon the partial pressure of the carbon dioxide regime under which the plants grow. Woodward proposed that the density of stomata measured on a leaf could be used as a proxy measure of fluctuations in atmospheric carbon dioxide in the past.

In 1987, Woodward published the results of an ingenious test of his method. We know that there has been an increase of about 20 per cent in the concentration of carbon dioxide gas in the Earth's atmosphere over the past 200 years. This figure has been calculated by direct measurements of gas trapped in air bubbles in ice cores from Antarctica. We also have samples of leaves from plants that grew under these changing atmospheric conditions. For over 200 years, botanists have been collecting plants and preserving them in herbaria in botanic gardens and museums. These specimens can be re-examined to investigate the effects of changes in key environmental parameters. Woodward was therefore able to count the density of stomata in seven species of temperate forest tree and one shrub in dried herbarium specimens, collected at intervals over the last 200 years. He then compared these measurements against the rise of atmospheric carbon dioxide over the same period. His observations demonstrated a 40 per cent decrease in the density of stomata from leaves in pre-industrial Britain to those in the same species growing today. The stomatal characteristics of a plant would therefore seem to be able to track the levels of carbon dioxide gas present in the atmosphere.

Since Woodward's initial work there have been many other observations and experiments that confirm this general trend, but some problems have also come to light. The sensitivity of the response varies with species, and it is not linear. The density of stomata is most sensitive to carbon dioxide values in the range of about 60 to 100 per cent of modern atmospheric levels. Also, stomatal density is sensitive to temperature, irradiance and water supply, all of which are factors that need to be considered carefully. In addition, the further back into the fossil record one extends this approach, the further removed one is from modern species in which responses to carbon dioxide can be calibrated experimentally. This introduces another layer of uncertainty. Despite these difficulties, early attempts at applying this method to the fossil record have provided promising results that are consistent with carbon dioxide concentrations inferred from other sources of data.

CLIMATE CHANGES

'The farther back you can look' wrote Winston Churchill 'the farther forward you are likely to see'. This aphorism has served the palaeoclimatologist well, as it has the historian, because long term trends or cyclical patterns of large amplitude might only be discernible when large chunks of the historical record are exposed to scrutiny. The botanical methods outlined above, in combination with other approaches that have been developed, especially in the fields of sedimentology, micropalaeontology and geochemistry, allow us to look back in time and to take the temperature of the Earth, so to speak, on a geological timescale. They enable us to place current climates within a very broad geological context, which we can use as a baseline with which to gauge the nature and scale of climate change in recent years.

THE LONDON CLAY

Underneath the busy metropolitan heart of the city of London is a geological formation known as the London Clay. From deep beneath the capital this stretches out under a large area of southern England, but the main outcrop forms a 200 km long and 50 km wide belt that emerges north east of London in the Essex marshes and runs in a south-westerly direction through the Thames Valley and into the western limb of the North Downs. In the London Basin, further major outcrops occur along the southern margin of the Thames estuary and along the coast neighbouring the Isle of Sheppey. As the name implies, the sediments are made up from poorly consolidated fine sands and clays, and where these rocks reach the surface they impart a heavy clay texture to the soils. The London Clay is famous for its fossils, including the remains of plants and animals. These provide evidence of an exotic subtropical flora from the Eocene (55–34 million years ago) in an area of southern England that today has a cool temperate climate.

Most of the fossil plants found in the London Clay are the fruits and seeds of flowers. Fragments of fern fronds and stems, as well as the leafy shoots and the cones of conifers, and wood derived from the trunks or branches of trees are also frequently encountered. During the Eocene, these bits and pieces were washed out from the shore and into a shallow sea, where eventually they sank to become fossilised in the sediments of the sea floor. Fossil plants have been collected from the London Clay for nearly 300 years, and in 1933 the flora

above: Treasure trove: fossil fruits from the London Clay, approximately 5-15 mm in diameter, preserved in 'fool's gold', (Eocene, Isle of Sheppey, England).

was monographed by Eleanor Reid and Marjorie Chandler. This involved the detailed description and naming of numerous species based on specially made collections of specimens that are now housed in the Natural History Museum, London. Importantly, all of the fossil species were compared to modern forms, which enables certain key environmental parameters to be deduced. It is this detailed taxonomic work that forms the framework for interpreting the environment of the London Clay.

Reid and Chandler were able to show that, of the numerous plant genera that have been recorded from the London Clay, about 143 can be assigned to modern families. About one-third of these can be classified into living genera, but all are considered to be extinct species. The climatic preferences of the plants are overwhelmingly tropical to subtropical. Over 90 per cent of the genera have nearest living relatives with a tropical distribution, and 18 per cent of these are known to be exclusively tropical. However, some elements of the flora are related to living groups that have both tropical and temperate distributions. Some 41 per cent fall into the latter category. Only 8 per cent of the flora have relatives that live today in the northern temperate climes. By investigating the climatic regime under which all of these different species could co-exist, we are able to draw some conclusions about the climate and environment of southern England during the Eocene.

The presence of an exclusively tropical element to the London Clay flora attests to a frostless climate in which rainfall was high and non-seasonal. It is also consistent with a high mean annual temperature that could have exceeded 25°C. On the other hand, the presence of temperate elements is more indicative of cooler conditions and some seasonality. The existence of seasonality is also corroborated by the presence of growth rings in the wood of about one third of the twigs examined. These observations point to a flora that was not fully tropical rainforest. The closest recent analogue is thought to be paratropical rainforest. This is predominantly evergreen, and grows in areas with a mean annual temperature of 20–25°C. Such forests are essentially frost-free, but temperatures can dip as low as −1°C. Nowadays, they are characteristic of coastal lowlands between 17°N and 26°N latitude in southern and eastern Asia. The coastal forest resembled a modern mangrove, which is an environment composed of trees and shrubs that are adapted to tidal land and capable of surviving inundation by salt water. Dominated by the *Nypa* palm, this forest fringed the coast and extended inland along a few large rivers. During the Eocene, this part of southern England would have borne a close resemblance to a river delta from the Indo-Malayan region of today.

above: Warmer times: London during the Eocene had a subtropical climate.

FEELING THE COLD

In 1773, during his exploration of the South Pacific and the Antarctic Oceans, Captain James Cook famously penned the following appraisal of Antarctica: 'I make bold to declare that the world will derive no benefit from it'. The ice-bound continent is today almost completely barren, but in the distant geological past it supported a diverse flora that included forests with both broad-leaved and coniferous trees. The fossil history of Antarctica tells of periods in Earth history when climates were much warmer and when forests flourished at much higher latitudes than they do today. Despite Cook's disparaging remarks, we now know that Antarctica affords an immeasurable wealth of data on ocean, atmosphere and climate. This last immense and unexplored region of the world continues to furnish challenges, and the exploration of the great southern continent is a major scientific endeavour in present times.

Our first inkling of the history of climate change in Antarctica came in 1892 when the Norwegian whaler Captain Carl Anton Larsen discovered fossilised wood on the Antarctic Peninsula. This was followed up by the Swedish Antarctic Expedition of 1901–1903, which was led by the famous explorer Otto Nordenskjöld's. In the annals of Antarctic exploration, the story of this Swedish expedition must surely rank among the most desperate and heroic. In February of 1902 Nordenskjöld's and five crew members disembarked to spend a winter on Snow Hill Island off the Antarctic Peninsula coast. The following season (1902/03 summer) their relief ship put a further three men ashore at Hope Bay. This second shore party was to make its way overland and sea ice to inform Nordenskjöld of the pickup point. The journey proved too difficult and, to make matters worse, the relief ship became trapped in pack ice and sank. Fortunately, its crew survived making their way to Paulet Island. So the ship's crew, Nordenskjöld's party and the second shore party were all forced to spend an additional winter in the Antarctic. Happily, the whole expedition was eventually rescued in 1903 by an Argentinian relief ship. During this time various elements of the expedition which included the geologist Johan Gunnar Andersson, collected fossil plants. These discoveries included a flora of Jurassic age from Hope Bay, Cretaceous wood and leaves from Snow Hill Island, and Cretaceous and Cenozoic plants from Cockburn and Seymour Islands. Following their return to Sweden, these collections were studied and the results published in a series of scientific articles by the palaeobotanists AG Nathorst, PKH Dusén, WUEF Gothan, and TG Halle from 1904 to 1913. These discoveries and the detailed scientific work that followed proved beyond a shadow of a doubt the existence of forests on Antarctica in the geological past.

Since the early days of Antarctic exploration, additional methods of studying climate history have been developed. These range from applications in palaeontology, to advances in sedimentology and geochemistry. The study of fossil wood, leaves and pollen can be used to infer temperature and rainfall parameters on land based on a combination of the nearest living relative method and leaf or wood structure. Evidence from the distribution and form of microscopic marine fossils such as foraminifera has also proved crucial. One important and widely used geochemical technique measures the ratio of two isotopes of oxygen (^{16}O:^{18}O) in limestone and

above: Fossil wood, approximately 9 cm long, collected from Antarctica by the ill-fated Terra Nova expedition, 1910-1913, led by Captain Robert Falcon Scott. *Antarcticoxylon priestlyi* (Permian).

the shells of marine animals. Oxygen isotopes and aspects of foraminifera form and distribution can provide estimates of sea water temperature, which is also a measure of climate change. Furthermore, the weathering of chemicals from sediments and sedimentary structures can furnish evidence for the waxing and waning of glaciers through time. More recently, it has been possible to use computers to develop models of climate change. Together, these diverse approaches tell a salutary tale of how climate change in Antarctica turned a once luxuriant forested landscape into an ice-bound wilderness, erasing higher life forms from an entire continent.

above: The barren wilderness of Seymour Island, Antarctica. The fossil plants found here testify to forests and warmer climates in Antarctica during the Paleocene and Eocene Epochs.

Geology and fossils both attest to a cooling trend in Antarctica over the last 90 million years from warm climates during the Late Cretaceous to present day glacial conditions. Analyses of fossil wood and leaves indicate that the mean annual temperature of the Antarctic Peninsula during the Mid to Late Cretaceous (88–78 million years ago) was 16–23°C. At that time the climate was warm, wet, and frost-free, and coniferous forests flourished. This was followed by considerable cooling towards the end of the Cretaceous, dipping to a low in the Paleocene. The transition from warm to cool temperate conditions was accompanied by a floristic change that saw conifers replaced as the dominant trees by flowering plants. By the Paleocene, the inferred mean annual temperature for the Antarctic Peninsula had dropped to 4–8°C, but there is no evidence for freezing conditions. Extrapolation of these temperature profiles further south onto the main continental landmass of Antarctica indicates that ice sheets could have formed near the pole at this time, especially at high elevations. This prolonged cooling trend was

above: Fossil preserved in carbonate nodule, approximately 15 cm long, shows that araucarian conifers formed part of the Eocene forests of Seymour Island, Antarctica.

temporarily reversed during the Late Paleocene and Early Eocene. Mean annual temperatures on the peninsula rose again to a high of 10–15°C, but by the Middle Eocene the cooling trend had resumed, and the climate was cold and wet, with a strong seasonal pattern of rainfall. In these respects, part of the Antarctic Peninsula would have resembled modern day southern Chile and Argentina. Evidence from sedimentology points to significant glaciation on the continent during latest Eocene to earliest Oligocene (34–30 million years ago). This was accompanied by a marked reduction in floral diversity, and ultimately the extinction of most higher life forms. Today, the modern flowering plant flora comprises just two species; *Colobanthus quitensis* (a cushion-forming member of the Caryophyllaceae) and *Deschampsia antarctica* (a prostrate tussock grass), both of which are found on the Antarctic Peninsula.

ICE AGE EARTH

The near complete eradication of higher plant and animal life on the Antarctic continent during the latter part of the Cenozoic sets the climatic context of the modern world. Despite recent global warming, attributed by many to the growth of industrial societies, we live in a world that is now dominated by ice. Looked at over the past few million years, the world is colder now than it has been since the end of the Carboniferous, over 290 million years ago. For at least 2.5 million years, Earth's climate has fluctuated between times of intense cold (glacials) and warmer periods (interglacials). During the coldest times, ice sheets expanded over large areas of North America and Europe, and much of the North Atlantic Ocean was covered by ice of one sort or another. Sea levels dropped by 100–150 m, exposing vast tracts of land, and bridging continents and islands that are today separated by marine barriers. Climatic zones were shifted equatorially by thousands of kilometres, and patterns of rainfall and aridity changed. Large swathes of present day desert were covered with vegetation. The last major glaciation came to an end about 10,000 years ago. During the warmer interglacial periods the ice retreated to more or less present day distributions, and Earth's climate took on its present form. But, even these warmer episodes are cool in comparison to the ancient hothouse conditions of the Mesozoic and early part of the Cenozoic.

The complex geological history of this ice age has taken a long time to unravel, and is still very much an active area of research, with a high degree of relevance to our understanding of the development of modern climates. Much of our information on climate change now comes from the measurement of oxygen isotopes (^{18}O and ^{16}O) in foraminifera. These are single-celled planktonic or benthic protists that live within shells, many of which are made from crystalline calcite. The fossilised remains of these shells can be recovered from cores drilled through sediments spanning millions of years of Earth history. The ratio of the two isotopes of oxygen within the calcite of the shell wall correlates with global temperature. By measuring the isotope ratios at different depths within a sediment core, one can build up a picture of temperature change through time. These data show that during the last 2.5 million years there have been many glacial and interglacial episodes of varying duration and intensity.

Much mystery surrounds the causes of the fluctuations in climate during the ice age, but most scientists now accept that changes in aspects of Earth's orbit around the Sun – so-called Milankovitch cycles – are the most likely triggering mechanism. The Milankovitch cycles are repeated patterns of change in the eccentricity, obliquity and precession of Earth on its orbit. The imprints of these cycles can be recognised in oxygen isotope graphs from deep-sea cores. In particular, orbital eccentricity, which affects Earth's distance from the Sun, varies in approximately 100,000-year cycles, and this correlates well with major pulses of glaciation during the last 900,000 years. By themselves, astronomical phenomena such as these are comparatively weak, and it is thought that in order to effect major climate change they need to be further amplified by other environmental factors (e.g. changes in atmospheric circulation or composition, changes in strength and path of ocean currents, expansion of snow covered areas). Today, much research is devoted to finding mechanisms by which the relatively weak astronomic signals are amplified to push us in and out of glacial episodes.

Sediments of glacial origin and those documenting the intervening interglacial episodes are draped across the surface of much of the northern part of the Northern Hemisphere. These are for the most part unconsolidated sands, mud or gravels, and frequently they are the first set of strata to be encountered during excavations for the foundations of buildings or the construction of roads. The fossils they contain can be difficult to distinguish from the shells or bones of living animals or from the carbonised remains of modern plants. Often though, the assemblages of bones and other bits and pieces unearthed will contain exotic elements that provide clues to their ancient origins. In the city of London, builders excavating foundations often encounter ancient deposits of the River Thames dating from an interglacial known as the Eemian or Ipswichian. This was a warm episode separating the last two ice ages and dating from about 130,000 to 115,000 years before the present day. Excavations for a sewer in Pall Mall in 1731 unearthed the molar tooth of an elephant at a depth of about 6.7 m. Since then, many mammalian bones have been found during building work in central London in the neighbourhood of the well-known landmark of Trafalgar Square. Animals represented include red deer and fallow deer as well as a whole menagerie of exotic species, such as a hippopotamus, an extinct straight-tusked elephant, a species of rhinoceros, a large wild ox and a lion. Many species of molluscs

above: Central London during the Ipswichian Interglacial (135,000–70,000 years before present) with hyena, elephant, hippopotamus, and lion.

have been collected, and some of these are today known only from rivers of southern Europe and north Africa. Likewise, of the over 150 species of fossil plants that have been documented, some hail from more southerly regions. The Water Chestnut (*Trapa natans*) is a floating aquatic plant with distinctive fruits. Today it is found throughout the Old World, and it has become naturalised in North America and Australia. In Europe, its natural distribution is much further south than London. The evidence from varied sources

above: Fruit of the water chestnut, *Trapa natans*, 2.5 cm in width, a southern European species common in the Ipswichian Interglacial of Britain (Mundesley, Norfolk, England).

therefore points to a warmer climate in the Eemian interglacial than at present in southern England. This warm episode peaked in the early part of the Eemian for a few thousand years, giving mid-latitude mean summer temperatures that are estimated to be about 2°C above those of today.

The fossilised remains of plants and animals provide some of the finest evidence for changes in climate through geological time. Historically, the concept of climate change arose through the study of rocks and the fossils and minerals they contained. Since the mid nineteenth century, scientists have been busy investigating, measuring and documenting extinct floras and faunas, and in so doing they have developed an invaluable database that attests to the dynamic nature of Earth's climate systems. Yet, the profundity and the extent of the changes they have discovered have only recently begun to make themselves felt in society at large. Climate change has finally become part of the political agenda. We must now seek to understand how longer term changes in temperature on a global scale will affect us, and we must identify the causes driving these changes. The fossil record provides us with one approach to measuring climate change and a method of gauging its effects. This is one way that fossil plants can be put to practical use in the service of humankind.

Chapter Six

PLANT LIFE
THROUGH THE AGES
· ·

AS SCIENTISTS BEGAN to make sense of the geological history of Earth and to dig up evidence for life in the past it became clear that the further one went back in time, the more dissimilar were the fossil organisms to those of the present day. In ancient rocks such as those of the Palaeozoic few fossils bear a close resemblance to living species. Moreover, the composition of the floras and faunas is radically different. Another striking fact is that there are fewer species in ancient rocks than in more recent ones. One of the clear messages to emerge from over 200 years of geological research is that species diversity has increased through time, as has the complexity of living things and their interactions. It is equally clear that this has not been a steady and uneventful progression. The inherent natural tendency of species to multiply has been curtailed from time to time. Major perturbations in the environment that took place over geologically short timespans resulted in the extinction of species on truly massive scales. It is changes such as these that mark the passing of geological time, giving to each age its own distinctive flora and fauna.

left: Jurassic landscape: woody gymnosperms were the major trees whilst ferns dominated the understorey and ground cover. Many of these plants are now extinct.

TAXONOMIC INFLATION

One approach to visualising the broad sweep of change in living things through the ages is to draw up a graph of the waxing and waning of taxonomic groups. One way that this has been

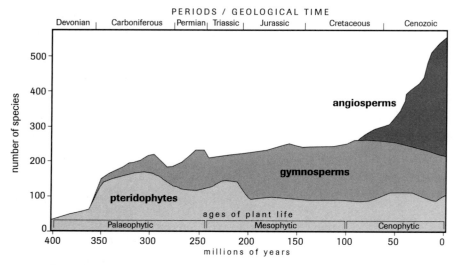

above: Taxonomic inflation: estimates of plant species diversity show an inexorable increase through geological time but the rate of increase is variable.

done is to tabulate for each species its first and last occurrence in the fossil record. The number of species at any given time can then be estimated, and the results plotted against geological time. In the 1970–1980s, three American palaeobotanists, Karl Niklas, Bruce Tiffney and Andrew Knoll, did just this for fossil plants, beginning their analysis at the dawn of life on land during the Silurian. The result was a running tally of the total estimated species diversity and how it breaks down into various groups; a graphical summary of plant evolution covering most of the Phanerozoic. Numerical analyses of this sort document intriguing patterns in the history of life.

One clear pattern to emerge is that the number of plant species has increased inexorably, but the rate of increase has varied substantially. During the early phases of life on land plant diversity was low. The rapid initial diversification of plants appears to have tailed off in the latter part of the Devonian. In the following Carboniferous there was a sudden change of tempo. A massive five-fold increase in species came about over a relatively short interval of time. This was again followed by a further lengthy period of slow and comparatively steady progression. Over the 200 million years, separating the Early Carboniferous from the mid-Cretaceous, calculations suggest that there was a total increase in species of a mere 20 per cent. Then the tempo of plant evolution picked up again. Things stepped up a gear, and there was another leap in diversity, beginning in the Late Cretaceous and continuing through to the present day. The taxonomic inflation that has characterised the Phanerozoic was made possible by the fact that the rate at which species evolve has exceeded by a small amount the rate at which they become extinct. One additional implication of this graph is that there is no reason to believe that we have reached an equilibrium level. The world of plants is not yet full. Left to itself, in the absence of interference by humans, plant species diversity looks set to increase.

A second clear message from the fossils is that different types of plant characterise different geological periods. So distinctive are these differences that geological time can be divided into three great ages of plant life. These have been dubbed the Palaeophytic (Silurian to Permian), the Mesophytic (Triassic to Early Cretaceous), and the Cenophytic (Late Cretaceous to present). Significantly, the three ages of plant life do not quite correspond to the threefold division of geological time into the Palaeozoic, Mesozoic and Cenozoic, a classification that is based on the fossil record of animals. The main differences are that the Palaeophytic commences with the development of conspicuous land floras in the Silurian, whereas the Palaeozoic encompasses the much lengthier record of marine animals reaching back to the Cambrian. Also, the boundary between the Mesophytic and the Cenophytic is earlier (mid-Cretaceous) than the corresponding boundary between the Mesozoic and the Cenozoic (Cretaceous/Tertiary boundary).

The oldest land floras are those of the Palaeophytic. These were dominated by plants such as ferns and clubmosses, as well as extinct species of the seed fern or cordaites type (see Chapter 4). Towards the end of the Carboniferous and in the early part of the Permian, half of all known plants were clubmosses. To put this into context, clubmosses represent much less than 1 per cent of plant species today. As the Palaeophytic gave way to the Mesophytic, the character of the land flora changed dramatically. The

above: The Mesophytic was the age of conifers. Petrified trunk of
Protocupressinoxylon purbeckensis from the Jurassic of Dorset, England.

above: Scale-like leaves of an extinct conifer *Cupressinocladus valdensis*, 7 cm long, from the Jurassic of Purbeck, Portland, England.

above: Thick, robust leaves of the extinct conifer *Pagiophyllum peregrynum*, branch 7 cm long, from the Jurassic of Lyme Regis, Dorset, England.

Mesophytic was the age of the conifers. These woody seed-bearing plants and their relatives, the cycad-like forms and ginkgos, were the most diverse groups. The shift from floras dominated by a spore-based reproductive strategy to one dominated by seed reproduction took place during the Triassic. From a botanical perspective, the modern era can be said to have commenced in the Late Cretaceous. This was the dawn of the age of flowers. Flowering plants first emerged during the Early Cretaceous, but it was in the latter half of the Cretaceous that they started to become a major constituent of species diversity. The contribution made by flowering plants has continued to rise steeply ever since. The modern world of flowers or the Cenophytic is the third great age of plant life.

What were the causes of these noteworthy increases in plant species diversity and the major changes in floral composition through geological time?

Was the rise of new groups somehow responsible for creating new species or were other factors at play in the environment? These are tricky questions to answer because of the difficulty of proving cause and effect in the geological past. One possible answer to the question of why diversity increases is ecological. As individuals become more numerous the demands placed on the resources that they need (e.g. space, light, water) become greater. This ecological climate favours specialisation, which is reflected in speciation. Another factor leading to greater species numbers might be the increasing complexity and diversity of resources brought about by the effects that plants themselves have on the environment. More species can mean more opportunities to diversify. For example, one cannot have a diverse flora of epiphytes without the large plants that make the canopies in which they thrive. In other words, diversity can feed upon itself to produce more diversity in a positive feedback loop.

Whatever the causes behind the steep increases in plant species diversity seen at certain times in the geological record, it is clear that not all of these correlate with noteworthy floristic changes. The rises in species numbers seen in the Early Carboniferous and again in a more sustained way during the Late Cretaceous and Cenozoic took place against very different backgrounds of floral change. During the Early Carboniferous there were increases across all major plant groups, although these were perhaps most marked in the seed-bearing types. In contrast, the sustained increases of the Late Cretaceous and Cenozoic were related to a massive development of one group in particular, the flowering plants. So great was the rise of this group that it even masked a parallel decline in the diversity of others, such as ferns. At other times, significant changes in floral composition did not go hand in hand with a steep rise in total species diversity. The diversification of conifers from the Permian through to the Jurassic is a case in point. This coincided with a very modest 9 per cent increase in plant species overall. Here the flourishing of conifers coincided with a marked decline in ferns and clubmosses, including the extinction of the tree clubmosses. It would seem that the conifers succeeded at the expense of other groups.

JURASSIC PARK

Certain periods of geological time have taken on special relevance because of the way that they have featured in the popular media. The Jurassic (206–144 million years ago) has become a high profile period because of its association with films and books about dinosaurs. In some respects, the Jurassic is symbolic of a time when strange (now extinct) animals and exotic plant life populated the Earth. So what do we know about the plants of the Jurassic and how different were the floras of that time to those of today?

The Jurassic was the mid point of the Mesophytic or the age of the conifers. During the Jurassic Earth's climate was warmer than today's. There is no evidence of glacial deposits, vegetation was well developed at high latitudes, and subtropical climates may have extended 60° north and south of the Equator. Evidence from the distribution of rocks that are indicators of climate, such as evaporites and coals, show that there was strong latitudinal variation in temperature and particularly in rainfall. Aridity was widespread in equatorial regions. In so far as one can circumscribe the vegetation of the Earth – which encompasses such an enormous range of habitats and climates – we can say that a very varied mixture of woody gymnosperms dominated the floras of the Jurassic (i.e. conifers, cycads and extinct relatives) alongside a herbaceous element comprising mainly ferns, horsetails and clubmosses. Flowers were completely absent from the Jurassic world.

above: The extinct gymnosperm *Caytonia* bore palmate leaves. Leaf of *Sagenopteris phillipsi*, 7 cm long, from the Jurassic of Cayton Bay, Yorkshire, England.

The coniferous constituent of Jurassic floras comprised large trees that can be classified within modern families such as Araucariaceae (Monkey-Puzzle family), Podocarpaceae (Yellow-Wood family), and Taxodiaceae (Redwood family). In addition to these and other more familiar forms there existed an extinct family of conifers called the Cheirolepidiaceae. This was a family of small trees and shrubs, most of which possessed diminutive scale-like leaves resembling those of modern trees in the cypress family. In others the main photosynthetic appendages were unbranched, cylindrical, succulent-looking shoots with thick cuticles and sunken or otherwise protected stomata. Leaf characteristics such as these are indicative of adaptation to water stress, and it is thought that Cheirolepidiaceae were particularly prominent in arid regions.

Whereas the extinct Cheirolepidiaceae are unmistakably conifers, other significant extinct groups are more difficult to place in relation to other gymnosperms. One such family is the Caytoniaceae. The habit of plants in this family is poorly understood, but at least some species may have been trees of small stature. Unlike modern gymnosperms, they bore palmate leaves. Their fruits were small and fleshy. Other groups of gymnosperms that were prominent during the Jurassic are the cycads and the extinct cycad-like Bennettitales. These bore a superficial appearance to palm trees with stout stems. Some were squat with unbranched, almost spherical or barrel-shaped trunks, whereas others were taller, sparsely branched shrubs or small trees. The barrel-shaped forms grew to between 0.5 and 3.0 m in height, but some of the tree-like forms might have grown to as much as 18 m. Most bore a crown of large, stiff, elongate pinnate leaves. Although cycads and Bennettitales are similar in many respects, fundamental difference in the structure of their cone-like reproductive organs indicate that the two groups are at best only distant relatives.

Ferns were a prominent component of the Jurassic landscape and many can be classified into modern families. In addition to the arborescent gymnosperms, tree ferns were a common part of the lower canopy. Large ferns in the families Osmundaceae, Matoniaceae, Dipteridaceae and Schizaeaceae were the most common herbaceous component of the ground cover. In general, ferns were most abundant in the more humid environments.

One of the best-known fossil plant assemblages from the Jurassic comes from the Middle Jurassic (about 180 to 165 million years ago) of Yorkshire, England. Here, some 260 species of plant have been described from more than 600 fossil-bearing levels, most of which are exposed along a stretch of coast between the towns of Scarborough and Middlesborough. Extensive excavations and collecting over long periods of time demonstrate how varied Jurassic floras were on a local scale. Floral composition changes from one site to the next, and this is attributable in part to local differences in environment of deposition as well as to real changes in plant communities through time. Scalby Ness is famed for the abundance of well-preserved *Ginkgo huttonii* leaves, but over 50 different plant species have been documented at this site.

above: Leaves of the extinct cycad–like Bennettitales, *Zamites gigas*, 40 cm long, from the Jurassic of Yorkshire, England.

In addition to *G. huttonii*, common conifer trees at Scalby Ness include species related to the Cheirolepidiaceae and the Podocarpaceae. Smaller stature gymnosperms included several Bennettittales and Cycadales. The most common ferns seem to have been tree ferns in the Dicksoniaceae. A much greater diversity of ferns and gymnosperms has been described from a little further along the coast at the Gristhorpe Plant Bed in Cayton Bay. In particular, this site is noteworthy for yielding the most important data on the extinct gymnosperm *Caytonia*. Hasty Bank – one of the few inland sites in which rocks of Jurassic age are exposed – has been interpreted as analogous to a modern mangrove. This abundance of different fossil plant sites in Yorkshire provides a unique insight into the floras and ecology of river and delta systems of Jurassic age.

LIVING FOSSILS

Modern gymnosperms are relics of the Mesophytic age, and some groups are so rare that they have come within a hair's breadth of extinction, only to be rescued at the last minute through the curiosity and intervention of humans.

above: Leaves of the Maidenhair Tree, *Ginkgo biloba*, a living fossil.

The family Ginkgoaceae today consists of a single species, *Ginkgo biloba* (Maiden Hair Tree). The leaves of the Ginkgoaceae are highly distinctive, and they are common fossils in Northern Hemisphere sediments of Jurassic and Cretaceous age. *Ginkgo biloba* was cultivated in China as a sacred tree in temple gardens and it was thought to be extinct in the wild until a small population was discovered in south east China in 1956. This tree is now widely planted as an ornamental, and it is also highly valued for its medicinal properties.

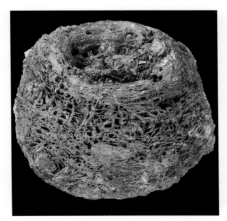

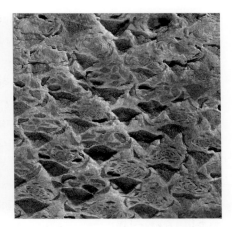

above: To nineteenth-century miners of Portland Stone, the barrel-shaped trunk of these cycad-like plants resembled giant fossil birds' nests. Trunk of the extinct Bennettitalean *Cycadeoidea microphylla*, 22 cm wide, from the Jurassic of the Isle of Portland, Dorset, England.

above: Flower-like cones embedded in the trunk of extinct cycad-like Bennettitales *Cycadeoidea saxbyana* from the Lower Cretaceous of the Isle of Wight, England.

right: Foliage of the Dawn Redwood *Metasequoia* was documented in the fossil record long before living specimens of these large conifers were discovered in the Chinese province of Szechuan in 1944. Foliage of *Metasequoia occidentalis*, 8 cm long (Paleocene/Eocene of Longyear Glacier, Spitsbergen, Norway).

Other types of conifers first came to light as fossils and only later were small living populations discovered. The foliage of *Metasequoia* (Dawn Redwood) was recognised in the fossil record for nearly a century before living specimens of this large tree were discovered in the Chinese province of Szechuan in 1944. More recently, in 1994, a new genus of Araucariaceae was established based on a handful of large trees growing in a deep gorge in the Wollemi National Park, Australia; a rugged mountainous region only 200 km north west of Sydney. The so-called Wollemi Pine (*Wollemia nobilis*) is very similar to fossil foliage found in the Mesozoic and Cenozoic sediments of Australia. Living fossils such as the Dawn Redwood and the Wollemi Pine are rare discoveries, but they do illustrate that small populations of even very large organisms can live in the vicinities of major cities and still remain unknown to science to the present day.

EXTINCTION OF THE MASSES

Despite the remarkable longevity of some lineages of plants, extinction is ultimately the fate of all species. The phenomenon of extinction, or the irreversible loss of species, was discovered in the 1700s when the unearthing of fossils brought to light species new to science. Naturally, the question arose as to whether the newly discovered fossils were dead representatives of living groups that had yet to be discovered in unexplored regions of the world or actual extinct organisms. Essentially, the argument hinged on proving a negative; the non-existence of the fossil form in the living flora and fauna. This is difficult to do, but at a meeting in Paris in 1769 the celebrated French polymath Baron Georges Cuvier hit on a good example. Presenting the results of a study of living and fossil elephants, Cuvier showed that many of his fossils were quite distinct species, and he argued convincingly that it was unlikely that living representatives of such large animals had remained undetected, even in the eighteenth century. We now know that the abundance of life on Earth masks an uncomfortable geological fact. To a rough approximation, of all the species that ever lived, less than 1 per cent are alive today.

A careful examination of the fossil record of any group of organisms reveals a continuous pattern of births and deaths of species through time. Set against this background pattern one can detect periods where the rate of extinction increased enormously. Where this increased rate was global in extent, where it covered a broad range of groups, and where it is known to have taken place over a short span of geological time, it is called a mass extinction. In addition to the loss of many species, a mass extinction is characterised by the eradication of high-level taxonomic groups such as families. Annihilation on this scale is clearly discernible in the fossil record. Such was the effect of the two largest mass extinctions that they mark the boundaries between the three major divisions of geological time. The largest known extinction of species occurred at the end of the Permian, at the boundary between the Palaeozoic and the Mesozoic. At this time, as many as 90 per cent of all species of marine invertebrates are thought to have become extinct. The most famous mass extinction – the one that administered the *coup de grace* to the dinosaurs – took place later at the boundary between the Cretaceous and Tertiary, which also marks the end of the Mesozoic.

Palaeontologists have learned much about the timing, the magnitude and the effects of mass extinctions by studying the fossil record of animals, in particular marine invertebrates. Marine sedimentary rocks provide a more continuous record of life on Earth than do those deposited in terrestrial settings, such as lakes and rivers, because they are more common and they accumulate in thicker sequences. Also, invertebrates often possess hardened outer parts such as shells and carapaces. Marine invertebrates therefore have among the most complete and extensive of fossil records. They have also been the subjects of innumerable taxonomic treaties, making them ideal models for investigating a host of historical phenomena. Less is known about extinction in plants, but it is apparent that most of the intense periods of extinction did not happen at the same time as those that affected animals.

Nine single or clustered peaks of extinction have been noted in the fossil record of plants since the Devonian. None of these coincides exactly with mass extinctions of marine invertebrates, and only two are associated with

above: Some conifers survived the mass extinction at the end of the Permian. Foliage of *Widdringtonites keuperianus*, block 13 cm long, from the Triassic of Keuper, Stuttgart, Germany.

extinctions among land-dwelling vertebrate animals (Early Triassic, Paleocene). Because the extinction peaks of plants and animals do not correspond in time, it seems likely that either the causes of the extinctions or the responses of these groups to mass extinction were very different.

The causes of mass extinction are still debated, and none is known for certain. Plausible scenarios encompass a very broad range of timescales from the more or less instantaneous to changes that would take place over tens of thousands or perhaps millions of years. On the slower acting end of the scale would be shifts in climatic regime at a global level or sea level fluctuations brought about by glaciation. Other possibilities include changes to the chemistry of the oceans, such as reduction in oxygen content or salinity. Much faster acting would be the effects of massive volcanic eruptions, or impacts from large meteorites or comets and other extra-terrestrial phenomena, such as radiation from supernovae and large solar flares. When observed through the lens of geological time in rocks that are hundreds of millions of years old, the instantaneous and catastrophic consequences of a meteorite impact can be difficult to distinguish from the longer acting effects of a glaciation.

Even though plants passed through the mass extinctions of marine invertebrates at the ends of the Palaeozoic and Mesozoic without losing an inordinately large number of species, it seems as though they did not escape completely unscathed. We have already seen that there are major differences between the floras of the Palaeozoic and Mesozoic. This floral transition was at first thought to coincide with the boundary between the Permian and Triassic, but this is no longer the case. Instead, the transition from Palaeophytic to Mesophytic floras is now known to have happened at different times in different parts of the world. It began first in Europe and North America during the early part of the Permian, but in eastern China similar changes did not make themselves felt until the the end of the Permian or the Early Triassic. The transition from Palaeophytic to Mesophytic floras began at low latitudes and over a global scale took 25 million years.

High resolution studies of the plant fossil record spanning the boundary between the Palaeozoic and Mesozoic provide evidence of significant ecological disturbance to plant communities as well as extinctions of species. Fossil pollen from sediments spanning the Permian/Triassic boundary in Europe tells a story of massive disturbance to tropical terrestrial ecosystems. This lasted some 4–5 million years, and it coincided with the extinction of the dominant conifers (Walchiaceae, Ullmanniaceae and Majonicaceae) of the latter part of the Permian. Conifer forests were replaced by more open vegetation of more shrubby and herbaceous aspect, where clubmosses of the quillwort type prevailed. When coniferous forests re-established during the early part of the Triassic, a different type of conifer (Voltiziaceae) became the dominant tree. A similar pattern has been observed at higher latitudes in Greenland, except that it involved different groups of conifers. Careful analysis of the pollen record shows that the extinctions in the gymnosperm tree component of the flora did not happen at the same time as the major extinction of invertebrates. There was a significant lag between the two events.

Some scientists think that mass extinction in plants coincided with periods of global climate change. There is some evidence to suggest that plant groups with certain life history traits seem to be affected by extinction in different ways at different times. It has been noted that during the Palaeozoic and the Mesozoic, ferns and clubmosses tend to have higher extinction rates than do the gymnosperms. One possible explanation is that this is related to the demise of humid swamp environments and the spread of generally more arid continental climates with the formation of Pangea during the Permian and Triassic. Gymnosperms reproduce by seeds, and are less dependent on the presence of water for reproduction than are ferns and their allies. The reverse appears to be true during the Tertiary, when gymnosperms seem to have borne the brunt of extinction in the face of ever increasing numbers of flowering plants.

GONDWANA

One of the enduring legacies of the famous voyages of discovery by Europeans of the eighteenth and nineteenth centuries was the collection and scientific description of plants and animals from around the world. These form the nucleus of the great collections in modern museums, and they have been responsible for a radical revision in the way that we perceive the structure of the Earth and the forces that have shaped its surface over time. As the fauna and flora from far flung lands came to be described and incorporated into the body of knowledge about the world, it was noted that there were some striking similarities among the living and extinct organisms of the Southern Hemisphere continents. In the 1840s, the English botanist Sir Joseph Dalton Hooker commented on the remarkable fact that the flora of South America and Australasia shared seven families of flowering plants and 48 genera that were not to be found elsewhere. Later, similar patterns were observed in other groups of plants and animals, such as liverworts, lichens, mayflies, midges and various types of vertebrates. How could one explain these similarities in view of the enormous stretches of ocean that separate the Southern Hemisphere continents today? One idea developed during the late nineteenth century was that there existed in the remote geological past a vast Southern Hemisphere continent. In other words, the modern continents of the Southern Hemisphere were somehow connected long ago, thus explaining the host of similarities in fauna and flora. The name given to this hypothetical continent was Gondwana, which is Sanskrit for land or forest of the Gonds; a people in north India.

One of the most distinctive fossil plants of Gondwana is called *Glossopteris*. This name comes from Greek, meaning 'tongue fern', which is a reference to the tongue-shaped leaves. When first described by the French palaeobotanist Adolphe Brongniart in 1828, *Glossopteris* was thought to be a type of fern, but now it is known to be a woody seed-bearing shrub or tree. The trunks of *Glossopteris* could reach 4 m in height, and they had a softwood interior resembling conifers in the Family Araucariaceae. Seeds and pollen-containing organs were borne in clusters at the tips of slender stalks attached to the leaves, but some species may have borne seeds in cones. It is thought that *Glossopteris* lived in a seasonal environment, and this is consistent with the occurrence of growth rings in the wood. Also, there is evidence that the plant was deciduous and that it grew under very wet soil conditions, like the modern Swamp Cypress (*Taxodium distichum*). The leaves of *Glossopteris* –

above: Some species of *Glossopteris* are known to have been small trees, which grew up to 4 m in height.

which can exceeded 30 cm in length – are common fossils in rocks of the Permian (290–248 million years ago) of India, Africa, South America, Australia and Antarctica.

At the time the hypothesis of Gondwana was conceived, the prevailing theory of the Earth saw continents as fixed in their relative positions. The problem of linking up the various elements of Gondwana was solved by hypothesising the existence of ancient land bridges. In 1912, this changed with the proposal of the theory of continental drift by the German meteorologist Alfred Wegener, an idea that was later developed and championed by the famous South African geologist Alex Logan du Toit. Wegener and du Toit argued that the continents are not fixed, rather they have moved or 'drifted' to their present day positions. In the past Gondwana was a single contiguous landmass composed of the present day Southern Hemisphere continents.

These ideas seemed incredible at the time, but in support of their theory Wegener and du Toit pointed to similarities in fauna and flora, and the distributions of fossils such as *Glossopteris* provided an important piece of evidence in the assembly of the Gondwana jigsaw puzzle. Wegener and du Toit also drew together other sources of evidence such as the remarkable geometric fit of South America and Africa, and similarities in rock age groups and types between adjoining areas of Southern Hemisphere continents that are now thousands of miles apart. The notion of drifting continents only became widely accepted in the 1960s, following the discovery of palaeomagnetism and the development of the theory of plate tectonics. Palaeomagnetism is the study of changes in polarity of Earth's magnetic field through time. The discovery of paired magnetic lineations in rocks either side of mid-oceanic ridges demonstrated that new oceanic crust was being created at the ridges. Plate tectonics is a revised theory of the Earth's surface and lithosphere, explaining the growth and movement of continents and other geological phenomena such as the origins of mountains and earthquakes. Gondwana is known to have been in existence for more than 500 million years, and through this long history changes in its distinctive flora have paralleled those in the Northern Hemisphere.

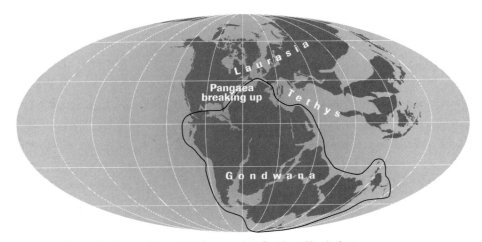

above: Gondwana (area circled): an ancient Southern Hemisphere supercontinent that fragmented to produce today's Southern Hemisphere landmasses (Jurassic).

DEEP FREEZE

Studies of the history of Gondwana show that the far reaches of this enormous continent experienced climatic regimes that ranged from warm humid equatorial rainforests, arid subtropical deserts, through temperate forests, to frigid polar ice caps. The approximate locations of major climatic zones have been worked out on the basis of lithological indicators such as coals, evaporites, bauxites and tillites as well as latitudinal evidence based on palaeomagnetism and the distribution of fossils. The climate of Gondwana was influenced by the size of the continent, its movement across latitudinal zones, and shifts in climate on a global scale from so-called 'hothouse' to 'icehouse' conditions. These changes had a major impact on the fauna and flora.

There is evidence of widespread glaciation in Gondwana during the Palaeozoic. Extensive ice sheets were a feature of the Late Carboniferous and the Early Permian. Ice sheets covered much of the continent, and they may have expanded to within 30° of the Equator. The onset of the Permo-Carboniferous glaciation coincided with the coalescence of Gondwana and the northern continents to form one huge landmass called Pangea. This reached its maximum development by the Middle Triassic. Gondwana in the Southern Hemisphere stretched from the South Pole to the Equator, and this was mirrored to the north by a somewhat less extensive assemblage of predominantly Northern Hemisphere continents. Continuity with other landmasses provided land-based pathways for biotic exchange, but this did not result in the immediate lessening in distinctiveness of the Gondwana flora. On the contrary, towards the end of the Permian *Glossopteris* gave way to another endemic group of trees and shrubs called *Dicroidium*. This was replaced by a more cosmopolitan flora of conifers and Bennettitales (cycad-like plants) towards the end of the Triassic. Although Jurassic floras were more cosmopolitan than those of preceding and succeeding periods, they still exhibit floral provisionalism. How Gondwana managed to maintain its distinctive flora during the development of Pangea is not fully understood. One possibility is that isolation of the Southern Hemisphere landmasses was bolstered by climatic zonation combined with the symmetric placement of Pangea about the Equator. Under this hypothesis, an equatorial belt formed a barrier to the exchange of temperate plants between the Northern Hemisphere part of Pangea and its Southern Hemisphere Gondwanan component.

BREAKING NEW GROUND

The similarities in the living and extinct plants and animals of South America, Africa, India and Australia noted by nineteenth-century scientists are consistent with the existence of Gondwana and its gradual fragmentation through the latter part of the Phanerozoic. The breaking apart of the supercontinent took place over about 150 million years. As ocean barriers formed, the plants and animals of newly formed continents became isolated from others to one degree or another and they developed their own distinctive indigenous characteristics. Thus, the floras of South America and Australia share groups derived from a common Gondwanan stock, but they also possess their own unique elements, many of which evolved after they became island continents. The splitting of Gondwana can explain much about the modern distribution of plants in the Southern Hemisphere, but evidence from the fossil record shows that this is not the whole story.

Detailed studies of the relationships of living species combined with a knowledge of the fossil record show that dispersal across ocean barriers as well as extinction are better explanations for the modern distributions of some species groups. Proteaceae (Proteas, Banksias, Grevilleas) is a prominent Southern Hemisphere family that contains over 1000 species. Recent phylogenetic studies based on DNA sequences point to a close relationship between some species from southern Africa and some of those from southwestern Australia. So close is this relationship that it is inconsistent with the ancient rifting of Africa from other elements of Gondwana. Long-distance dispersal is therefore a more probable explanation for the distributions of these particular species. Similar sorts of argument have been used to explain the modern distributions of other groups, such as the Casuarinaceae (She Oaks, River Oaks) of the Indo-Pacific region. It seems likely that dispersal across ever widening ocean barriers would have been more important during the earlier stages of the rifting of Gondwana.

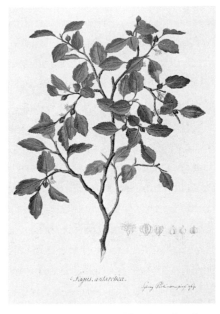

The processes of regional extinction through climate change and modification of landforms is also a consideration in explaining the distributions of plants in the Southern Hemisphere. A wide belt of *Nothofagus* (Southern Beech) forest is thought to have covered landmasses of Gondwana during the Paleogene 65–24 million years ago. Today this forest is still extensive in parts of

above: Extensive forest of Southern Beech, *Nothofagus antarctica*, covered large tracts of Gondwana during the Paleogene. Drawing made by Sydney Parkinson on Cook's first voyage (1768-1771).

Australia, Tasmania, New Zealand and the highlands of Southeast Asia and South America. The occurrence of a subgenus of *Nothofagus* called *Brassospora* in New Guinea and New Caledonia seems to suggest that these islands once had a close geological relationship. But, evidence from the fossil record shows that *Brassospora* was much more widely distributed through southern Gondwana during the Paleogene. Extinction on a regional scale has narrowed the distribution of *Brassospora*. From this perspective, the modern representatives in the islands of New Caledonia and New Guinea are probably indicative of recent colonisation from separate areas and parental stock.

Nobody knows how many species of plant are alive today, but conservative estimates place the figure in excess of 300,000 species worldwide. This rich diversity exists because, in the longer view of things, the rate at which new species originate exceeds the rate at which they become extinct. Why one species or larger taxonomic group should fall rapidly whereas another will succeed for a lengthy period of time is largely unknown, although plausible reasons can be given in well-studied cases. The diversity of plants and the floristic similarities and differences among regions are explicable in part by variation in physical parameters of the environment, such as climatic regime. Also significant is the restless nature of the Earth's surface. The seemingly solid stage upon which life's drama is acted out is actually in motion. Continents have rifted apart only to collide with others and to rift apart again over hundreds of millions of years. Sea levels have risen and fallen in response to glaciation, creating islands or conversely causeways between isolated lands. In this way, regions that have been evolving in isolation are brought together and species are forced into new competitive relationships. In addition to competing with each other, plants have had to contend with the ever zealous attentions of animals. It is to this subject that we turn in the next chapter.

Chapter Seven

PLANTS AND ANIMALS
· ·

ANIMALS ARE RELIANT ON PLANTS, and most animals interact with them on a daily basis. Plants are looked upon as sources of food, but many animals also make them their homes, typically living inside bark, wood or leaves, or simply using trunks and branches as places on which to build. These exploits can be costly, and strenuous measures are taken to fend off herbivores and others intent on pilfering hard won supplies of sugars and nutrients. Frequently, plants are able to turn the tables on their unwitting animal guests to further their own ends, using them as agents of dispersal or as pollinators. The most varied and numerous of these contacts are with the arthropods, and this relationship is also by far the oldest. Others that have engaged with plants in many ways include mammals, reptiles, birds and dinosaurs. These interactions are by their very nature dynamic, and they are seldom captured in the freeze frame of the fossil record. We do however have much to learn from studying the appearance of organisms, both living and fossil. The stories of battles fought and the tales of alliances forged can often be read from form and function. Also, evidence of interactions can manifest themselves in other ways, such as damage of a particular sort or reactive growth of a peculiar type. Such things fall within the purview of the fossil record, where they leave a set of clues for

left: Fossil cockroach testifies to the evolution of flight during the Carboniferous Period. *Phyloblatta brongniart* approximately 4 cm in length, from Commentry (Allier), France (Late Carboniferous).

the palaeontologist to follow. Building up a picture of how plants and animals have interacted in the past therefore draws on evidence from very varied sources.

LIFE IN THE LITTER

Plants and animals are known to have co-existed on land for over 400 million years, and the earliest direct evidence for interactions comes from the Rhynie Chert, which is a fossilised hot springs system of Early Devonian age (Chapter 1). At Rhynie, all of the animals were tiny arthropods, and at least six different groups are known. These included relatives of modern day spiders (trigonotarbids), centipedes, mites, springtails (collembolans), freshwater crustaceans, and an enigmatic extinct group that show similarities to both crustacea and insects (euthycarcinoids). These animals dwelt within the litter of decomposing plant stems at the soil surface. Trigonotarbids have

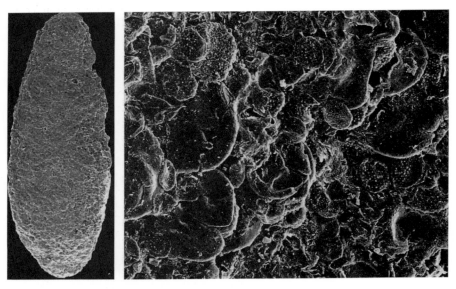

above: Fossilised faecal pellets, also known as coprolites, are one source of evidence for the diet of early land-dwelling arthropods. Coprolite (left), approximately 3 mm long, and enlargement (right), showing mass of plant spores (Earliest Devonian, Shropshire, England).

been seen inside cavities within stems and also tucked away inside empty spore sacs. Since trigonotarbids were most likely predators, it seems probable that they entered natural chambers within the plants for purposes other than seeking food. One possibility is that they were in search of a refuge for moulting. At Rhynie we find the earliest direct evidence for animals using plants for shelter.

above: Eye to eye: head on view of the mite *Protacarus crani* from the early Devonian Rhynie Chert. The legs are the most discernable elements in this image. Size approximately 300–450 μm long.

Many of the arthropods of the Rhynie Chert were predators. We know this because their diet can sometimes be inferred from the shape and form of the mouthparts, and inferences can also be drawn from the relationships of the fossil species to living groups whose diet is known. The Rhynie Chert and other Early Devonian plant sites provide some of the earliest evidence of plants being used as sources of food. Some of this is circumstantial. Many early plants possessed tiny cuticular hairs or larger spine-like hairs. It is conceivable that these formed a physical barrier, repelling arthropods, as do the hairs in modern species of plant. Hairs or spines of this sort were probably most effective during juvenile stages of growth when they would have formed a dense, bristly covering. Other evidence is more direct, and comes in the form of physical damage to the plants themselves. This has been observed in anatomical preparations of petrified stems, which sometimes exhibit wounds that give the appearance of puncture damage. Wounds of this sort can be made by the piercing mouthparts of sap-feeding arthropods. Still further evidence comes from fossilised faecal pellets (coprolites). These are quite abundant and can be recovered by dissolving rock in hydrofluoric acid. The faecal pellets contain almost exclusively spores. On the face of it, this would seem to be consistent with a diet of spores, but it might also reflect the resilience of spores in the digestive system of arthropods. In addition to these types of evidence, a fossil millipede has been found recently at Rhynie with spores and other plant fragments preserved in the gut. Taking all of the evidence into account, scientists think that the non-carnivorous element of early arthropod faunas was, on the whole, feeding on dead plant remains. In other words, the early plant-eating arthropods were in fact detritus feeders rather than true herbivores. Early food chains would therefore seem to have been sustained principally through arthropods foraging on the dead and decomposing remains of the vegetation in which they lived.

HERBIVORY – EATING WELL IN THE FOSSIL RECORD

Arthropods continued to provide the first effective link in the terrestrial food chain throughout the Devonian and for most of the Carboniferous. This was accompanied by the development of true herbivory – here defined as feeding on living green parts or bark – probably during the early part of the Carboniferous. Digesting living plant material is a tricky business because animals lack the enzymes capable of breaking down cellulose, which is the primary constituent of plant cell walls. For arthropods feeding on leaf litter this is not so much of a problem because decomposition brought about by soil micro-organisms is already underway. Animals that feed on living plants need to cultivate within their guts a flora of microbes that is capable of aiding in the breakdown of cellulose. It seems likely therefore that herbivorous arthropods evolved from ones that fed on litter following the recruitment of microbial allies and their adaptation to life inside the gut.

above: Bored seed, approximately 12 mm in width. Marks and scars on fossil plants document increasingly sophisticated methods of feeding by arthropods. *Trigonocarpus parkinsoni* (Late Carboniferous, England).

By the latter part of the Carboniferous, the land fauna had become much more diverse. A variety of winged insects had evolved, including grasshopper-like species and cockroaches. The menu for arthropods had broadened to include sap feeding, the eating of pollen and spores, the boring of seeds and wood, and possibly also marginal leaf feeding and leaf mining. Evidence for these activities can be adduced from faecal pellets and less often from fossilised gut contents. This indicates that spore eating preceded leaf feeding. One source of evidence for the latter comes in the form of physical damage to the leaves themselves, but this is comparatively rare. It has been calculated that only 4 per cent of leaves of Late Carboniferous age

above: Frayed edges to leaf tips of a seed fern tell of troubled times. Damage of this sort might be caused either by post-mortem decay or through arthropod feeding. *Neuropteris*, block approximately 12 cm long (Late Carboniferous, Writhlington, near Radstock, Somerset, England).

show any evidence of leaf feeding. This physical evidence needs to be interpreted carefully though. For one thing, it is difficult to rule out post mortem damage such as decay. Also, the feeding traces of land snails can be difficult to separate from those made by arthropods. The vertebrates – which had evolved land-dwelling forms during the latter part of the Devonian – were still carnivorous or insectivorous. Vertebrate herbivores did not begin to make a significant impact on plant life until the Permian.

What sort of a response did this onslaught from the arthropods provoke in plants? This question is not easy to answer conclusively, because establishing cause and effect in the geological past can be difficult. Beginning in the latter part of the Carboniferous, there is evidence for the development of sophisticated mechanical and possibly chemical defences against arthropods. One sees the appearance of fibrous and woody tissues in the walls of seeds, pollen and spore-bearing organs. These would have acted as barriers against mechanical damage, shielding plants from biting or probing mouthparts. Perhaps the very large size of some seeds discouraged ingestion by small arthropods. Certain plants, in particular the medullosan pteridosperms (Chapter 4), disgorged resins in response to wounding, whereas others, such as the marattialean tree ferns (Chapter 4), exuded mucilage, both of which would have aided in repelling physical attack by arthropods. Others bore microscopic glandular trichomes on the under surface of their leaves. These are hairs that comprise a stalk topped by a large secretory cell. Like in modern forms, the function of the secretory cell was to release a sticky liquid when triggered by physical contact with an arthropod limb. These microscopic secretions are powerful enough to cement an arthropod

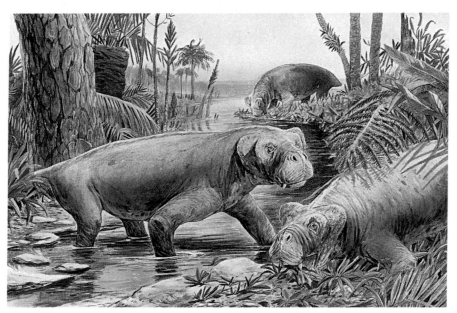

above: Early vertebrate herbivores were quadrupeds of low stature and could not reach into the crowns of large trees. *Lystrosaurus* (Early Triassic).

to the leaf surface. By the end of the Carboniferous, arthropods had been co-evolving with plants for over 130 million years, leading to an enormously varied set of interactions and responses in the biology of both groups.

Herbivorous vertebrates evolved from carnivorous or insectivorous ones, and scientists have calculated that this transition took place independently in perhaps as many as eight different lineages during the Permian. Unlike the arthropods, most information on vertebrate herbivores comes from clues in the skeleton and the dentition of the animals themselves. One reason that fossil plants are not such an effective source of information in this case is because vertebrate herbivores are big browsers with huge appetites. They don't nibble away at the edges of leaves, and they are not small enough to live within plants. They are bulk processors of vegetation on a grand scale. Vertebrate herbivory came to the fore at a time of flora change during which seed-bearing plants began to flourish in seasonally arid areas. The foliage of conifers and cycadophytes in particular was adapted to resisting the effects of seasonal drought and therefore was very robust. It would have posed formidable problems to the digestive system of any animal. Also, many of these plants were tall, yet the early vertebrate herbivores were quadrupeds of low stature, browsing within a metre or so of the ground. Much of the foliage of mature trees was therefore out of reach. The brunt of the browsing was borne by low stature vegetation such as the seedlings of large trees, herbaceous ferns, horsetails and the smaller shrubby pteridosperms.

DINOSAURS AND BIRDS

Things took a turn for the worse for plants in the Late Triassic and Jurassic with the advent of herbivorous dinosaurs. These were some of the most formidable vegetarians that the world has ever seen. Beginning with the prosauropods in the Late Triassic and culminating with the truly giant sauropods of the Late Jurassic, dinosaurs became bigger and more effective browsers with the passage of time. The prosauropods had long necks, and were able to support themselves on their hind legs in order to reach up trees. The effect of this was that browsing height jumped from 1 to 6 metres. The giant sauropods of the Late Jurassic had giraffe-like necks enabling them to reach even further (up to 12 m) to feed in the crowns of trees. A fully-grown *Brachiosaurus* could have measured as much as 23 m in length and weighed 20 to 30 tonnes. The unprecedented height of these sauropods opened up a new source of vegetation to browsing vertebrates, but sustaining their huge bulk depended on ready access to vast quantities of fodder. It has been estimated that the larger sauropods could have consumed 200 kg of food a day. During the Jurassic dinosaurs rose to the challenge set by plants by growing to very large sizes, and the consequence for trees is that they became vulnerable to browsing over a much greater length of their life cycle.

Just as the increasing height of vertebrates opened up new opportunities for browsing, so did parallel developments in food processing. Like the arthropods, vertebrates have a problem digesting plants because they are unable to break down cellulose. They too must rely on physical processing of plant material combined with playing host to colonies of gut-adapted microbes to make up for their enzyme deficiencies. This is reflected in many aspects of dinosaur anatomy and behaviour.

Dinosaurs developed an impressive range of oral processing techniques including pulping, grinding, slicing, puncturing and crushing. Some had powerful jaw muscles and cheeks – a feature elsewhere known only in mammals – to aid the back teeth in crushing and grinding. All ornithischians boasted sharp horny beaks of one sort or another that would have been effective tools for cropping plants. *Iguanodon* and the hadrosaurs had broad beaks, and these animals were probably general browsers. Leaves and twigs cropped by the beak were passed back to arrays of interlocking sharp-edged cutting teeth with broad grinding surfaces. On the downward bite the teeth met at a steep angle forcing the upper jaws outwards. This created a grinding motion that shredded the cropped plants. The ceratopians such as *Triceratops* had a narrow hooked beak rather like that of a parrot. This would have been suited to cutting rather than cropping or browsing. The jaw bore hundreds of interlocking teeth, and these had a slicing rather than grinding action. Smaller ornithischians had narrower beaks more suited to precision feeding and although some evidently ground their food, others had rows of simple diamond-shaped teeth in the back of the jaw. This latter arrangement is indicative of feeding on softer nutritious food that required less substantial processing. It is probable that the smaller ornithischians made a greater investment in selective foraging, seeking out fruits and seeds.

Paradoxically, the biggest plant eaters of all, the sauropods, had little in the way of oral processing skills. The heads of these animals were comparatively small, and their mouths were lined with teeth that were unable to grind or to chew food. In some the teeth were diamond-shaped or spoon-shaped with sharp edges suited to tearing and biting off leaves and twigs, whereas others had 'tooth combs' that stripped the foliage away. How then did these giants manage to extract the vast quantities of carbohydrates and nutrients they needed from the plants that they ate? The answer is that the head and teeth were

above: Gastroliths (stomach stones): some large dinosaurs swallowed stones that lodged in the stomach, aiding the process of digesting plants through a milling or grinding action. The largest stone depicted measures slightly more than 7 cm.

simply a cropping tool. Their purpose was to gather food. Leaves, twigs, cones, etc. were stripped from the trees and swallowed whole. In these beasts, the real business of food processing began in earnest in their guts.

Occasionally, within or close to the skeletons of suaropod dinosaurs one can find piles of angular polished stones. These curious objects are gastroliths or stomach stones, and they provide direct evidence that sauropods had a gastric mill similar to the gizzard of modern birds. In addition to eating plants, sauropods would occasionally have sought out and swallowed pebbles. These stones lodged in the stomach where they were used to pound and grind plants. During feeding, cropped plant material would have passed down the long neck and into the stomach, and it was here that most of the food processing was done. The stomach was powerfully muscular, and it milled unprocessed plant material in a potent mix of digestive enzymes and stones. The indigestible remnants would then pass on to the intestine where they would spend time in a series of pouches packed with microbes that facilitated further breakdown of the cellulose through fermentation. When no more nutrients could be extracted, the remnants passed out of the body as droppings.

In much the same way that plants have evolved defences against arthropods, the rise of large vertebrate herbivores during the Mesozoic is likely to have triggered further developments aimed at discouraging very large

above: Like modern cycads, the extinct Bennettitales had tough foliage. Reconstruction of *Williamsonia sewardiana* (Jurassic).

above: Fond of fruit: the ribcage of this early bird conceals numerous large seeds that formed the stomach contents at time of death. Skeleton of *Jeholornis prima* from the Early Cretaceous of Chaoyang City, western Liaoning, China.

browsers. So, how does one fend off a 20 tonne sauropod dinosaur with a large appetite for leaves? One possibility is that subtle mechanical and chemical mechanisms would have been brought into play. We know from our experience in the present day that plants can make themselves unpalatable or difficult to digest. Being more distasteful than your neighbour is probably all that it takes to redirect the attention of even the largest of general browsers. We know that the leaves of many Mesozoic trees and shrubs were thick. This is thought to have been an adaptation to aridity, but it may also have served the plants well by making them less palatable and more difficult to digest. Some araucarian conifers have very tough leaves that extend onto branches presenting a spiny surface barrier to damage-prone parts of the tree. The leaves of cycads are also very tough, and when they die they can drop to form a thorny defensive skirt to the vulnerable growing part of the trunk. Living cycads have toxic foliage and seeds, and it is tempting to attribute this to their long interactions with herbivores. Unfortunately, the efficacy and ubiquity of chemical and even mechanical defences are impossible to judge from the fossil record.

Most palaeontologists now group birds within dinosaurs because of the many lines of evidence that point to a close relationship from skeletal morphology to feathers. Scientists thought that early birds were on the whole insectivorous, but recently evidence has been unearthed that some at least ate fruits and seeds as part of their diet. One of the earliest examples of an arboreal plant-eating vertebrate comes in the shape of a fossil bird from the famous Jehol Biota of north east China (Early Cretaceous). *Jeholornis prima* was somewhat larger than a pigeon and fully capable of powered flight. It resembled modern birds in many features, but one noticeable difference is that it possessed a long skeletal tail. This is one of a number of features that place *Jeholornis* in an intermediate position between non-avian theropod dinosaurs and modern birds. One of the most intriguing features of *Jeholornis* is that dozens of large fossilised fruits or seeds (8–10 mm long) were found preserved within the chest area. These were surely part of the contents of the stomach prior to death. Seeds, like bones, are comparatively robust objects,

above: Details of seeds, up to 1 cm long, found in the stomach region of the early fossil bird *Jeholornis prima* from the Early Cretaceous of Chaoyang City, western Liaoning, China.

so they have become fossilised whereas the soft tissues of the bird have long decomposed. The intact state of preservation of these seeds means that they were swallowed whole for processing within the gut rather than crushed within the beak. Furthermore, the number of seeds (over 50) is evidence that the bird possessed a large crop. *Jeholornis* presents the earliest direct fossil evidence of seed eating in Mesozoic birds.

We know from its anatomy that *Jeholornis* was capable of flight and that it had some ability to move in trees or to climb. Like many modern birds it may well also have spent time on the ground. We do not know which of the main groups of plants *Jeholornis* fed upon for its last meal because the state of preservation of the seeds is not good enough to make a precise taxonomic diagnosis. It seems likely though that the seeds belonged to a gymnosperm of one sort or another. Also, we cannot know for sure whether the seeds came from a small shrub or a large tree, or indeed whether they were plucked from the branches or scavenged from the ground after being shed. This means that although we know that *Jeholornis* fed on seeds, we cannot say for sure whether it browsed in the canopy.

THE UPS AND DOWNS OF MAMMALS

Dinosaurs were unquestionably the pre-eminent plant-eating vertebrates of the Mesozoic, and following their demise at the end of the Cretaceous there was a significant hiatus during which very large herbivores were absent from the land altogether. Nearly all plant-eating dinosaurs subsisted predominantly on foliage and to a lesser extent on fruits and seeds. During the Cenozoic the mammals slowly laid claim to the roles of large general browser and fruit eater, but even the biggest herbivorous mammals never attained the enormous proportions of the sauropod dinosaurs. Unlike dinosaurs, mammals also diversified to exploit a far greater range of plant eating possibilities. There are aquatic herbivorous mammals, small ground-dwelling browsers, specialists in grasses and the like (grazers), as well as numerous forms that have taken to the trees and to the skies. With the exception of the birds, dinosaurs never quite exploited this diversity of environments or range of plant resources.

As with other vertebrates our knowledge of what fossil mammals ate comes principally from inspecting the form and arrangement of their teeth. This is just as well, because teeth are by far the commonest fossils. Cranial and postcranial skeletons are rare, yet information on the latter in particular is important in determining how a mammal moved and whether it lived on the ground or in the trees. It is also possible to obtain information about a mammal's diet using the nearest living relative approach. In much the same way that one can estimate the climatic tolerance of a fossil plant by knowing how it is related to living species (Chapter 5), one can use knowledge of relationships to obtain an independent assessment of the diet of a mammal. If the closest living relatives can be determined with confidence and they are all known to eat fruit, then it is likely that the fossil was a fruit eater too. Caution is required though because diet can change within families. A good example is horses. In the Eocene they fed on fallen fruit and the leaves of low stature shrubs and forbs (broad-leaved herbs). Today they are grazers. Exceptionally, such as in the famous Middle Eocene oil shale of Messel (near Darmstadt, Germany) one can find entire mammals with their gut contents preserved.

Today many herbivorous mammals are general browsers and grazers that are capable of processing large quantities of foliage. Not so in the early days of mammal evolution when all plant eaters specialised in fruit. The earliest mammals come from the Late Triassic, and even though these were mostly small insectivores it is likely that some included fruit in their diet. Evidence from fossil teeth shows that fruit eating became more of a speciality through the Late Jurassic and the Cretaceous. The most important of the fruit-eating mammals of the Mesozoic was an extinct group of rodent-like critters called the multituberculates. Some of these had teeth suited to crushing, whereas in others the incisors were more suited to gnawing. Hard dry seeds were probably a component of their diet. The only other group of plant-eating mammals known from the Late Cretaceous are the opossum-like marsupials, but these were less specialised, eating both insects and fruit.

Fruit eating in mammals increased through the mass extinction at the end of the Cretaceous and into the Paleocene. During the Paleocene, the multituberculates were joined by the plesiadapiforms. This extinct group contained the close relatives of the primates. Some of their members were highly adapted to life in the trees, and evidence from dentition indicates that fruits and seeds were part of their diet. Most other plant-eating Paleocene mammals belong to the condylarths, which is a group that contains the ancestors of the hoofed mammals of today. The evidence from both arboreal and ground dwelling species shows that the plant-eating mammals of the Late Cretaceous and the Early Paleocene subsisted on a diet of fruits and seeds, augmented in some cases by insects. Fruit eating preceded the evolution of mammals capable of consuming foliage, presumably because fruits are more easily processed through the digestive system. The fruit eating proclivities of early mammals also paved the way for their exploitation by plants as agents of seed dispersal.

Fruit-eating mammals of the Late Cretaceous and Early Cenozoic diversified into ground dwelling and arboreal forms, and by the Eocene some of these were airborne. Rodents are today an important group of fruit eaters, and they tend to specialise in feeding on hard dry fruits. The rodents first appeared in the Late Paleocene, and they diversified during the Eocene into

above: Paleocene mammal from North America: *Taeniolabis* was a small rodent-like animal about the size and weight of a beaver. It was herbivorous with sharp gnawing teeth.

an astonishing range of forms that encompassed very large and small ground dwellers, climbers, arboreal and even gliding species. Tree dwelling animals diversified during the Paleocene with the arrival of the arboreal plesiadapiforms and their close relatives the primates. True primates are today among the most important of the arboreal fruit eaters, and they first appeared in the fossil record at the boundary between the Paleocene and the Eocene. Early members were probably insectivores, but by the Middle Eocene many primates were eating fleshy fruits. The main airborne fruit-eating mammals of today are the fruit bats. These first appeared in the Late Eocene, and they probably also had insect-eating forebears. By the end of the Paleocene, and possibly earlier, fruit and seed-eating mammals were well established in the treetops.

Since fruit eating is such an early innovation in mammals, and since many of the fruits that they ate came from the flowering plants, could the evolution of these two groups be linked? When one examines the dimensions of fruits and seeds and plots the changes in these variables against time there is a clear trend towards increasing size beginning during the latter part of the Cretaceous (approximately 80 million years ago) and continuing through to the end of the Paleocene. One explanation for this increase in fruit size is that it was driven by the appearance of animals capable of acting as dispersal agents. This hypothesis emphasises the availability of suitable seed-dispersing animals as the principal factor controlling fruit size. Conversely, changes in vegetation might have been driving the evolution of mammals. One plausible alternative argument is that changes in world climate around the boundary between the Cretaceous and the Paleocene promoted the development of denser, more complex forests and this sort of environment favoured the larger fruits and seeds. Climate change was therefore driving changes in vegetation that caused further changes in seed dispersal. Fruit-eating mammals and birds were the beneficiaries of these changes, not the agents. Deciding between competing theories of this nature can be difficult because using fossils one can show at best only correlations between the appearance and disappearance of groups through time. Demonstrating causes and effects is an altogether more difficult matter and must draw on additional arguments, such as those developed form observations of the ecology of living organisms.

ARTHROPODS – AN ENCORE

While plant-eating vertebrates diversified during the Mesozoic Era, the arthropods continued to increase in number and importance, showing a readiness and ability to exploit plants that is unmatched by other animals. Many major groups of insects containing herbivorous species expanded during this time. These include Hymenoptera (ants, wasps, bees), Diptera (true flies), Coleoptera (beetles), Hemiptera (true bugs), Thysanoptera (thrips), Orthoptera (grasshoppers), Ephemeroptera (mayflies), and towards the latter part of the Mesozoic Era, Lepidoptera (moths, butterflies). Many of these groups left their mark on plants, feeding on leaves, wood, and the like. Others came to be exploited by plants in their pollination biology. Most arthropod feeding strategies have ancient roots, with many common modern forms recognisable in fossil plants of the Palaeozoic. It is also probable that most strategies evolved independently perhaps many times in different lineages. Arthropods continually reinvented or rediscovered similar ways of feeding on plants throughout subsequent periods of geological time.

Insect damage induced by feeding or through sheltering is commonly observed in fossilised plants, where it can take numerous forms. In the flowering plant dominated floras of the Late Cretaceous and Cenozoic, approximately 30 distinct types of external foliage-feeding can be recognised. Some insects nibble away at the margins of leaves, whereas others make holes in the surface. Other forms of feeding behaviour are highly stereotyped and can result in intricate patterns. Invasive feeding by insects through piercing and sucking is less easily recognisable in fossils, but there are sporadic records dating back to the Devonian Period. Another form of invasive feeding at which arthropods excel is the construction of tunnels through resilient plant tissues such as wood and bark. The boring of hard parts is a speciality of oribatid mites, termites, and holometabolous insect larvae. Oribatid mite borings are well documented in fossils of the Late Carboniferous. It is generally accepted that insect-size borings appear somewhat later during the Permian Period, and by the Mesozoic some of these are attributable to beetles. Bark-beetle damage is first encountered much later, during the early part of the Cretaceous. Another form of tunnelling takes place within the tissues of the leaf. Some arthropods live in the confinement of the interior of leaves, sandwiched between the upper and lower epidermises. These so-called leaf miners are mainly the larvae of holometabolous insects and more rarely mites. Leaf-mining is one of the few forms of herbivory that may actually have originated during the Mesozoic.

Another common indicator of arthropod feeding is the presence of galls. These aberrant growth forms are induced by the presence of an arthropod living within the tissues. Typically, galls are induced by larval or nymphal stages of the life cycle. Today, about 80 per cent of galls are on leaves, but the earliest forms are found on the stems and petioles of plants growing in the coal swamps of the latter

above: A 'leaf miner' has left a snaking trail in this leaf from the Middle Eocene of Bournemouth, England.

part of the Carboniferous. It seems likely that this feeding strategy is derived from boring or tunnel-making precursors.

Looking for fossil evidence of insect damage to leaves requires an abundance of well-preserved fossils, and one of the best places to begin one's search is at the Florissant Fossil Beds National Monument of the US. Situated high up in the Rocky Mountains, some 40 km west of the town of Colorado Springs, Florissant is famed for its fossil plants and insects that date from the latest part of the Eocene Epoch, some 34 million years ago. The fossilised leaves of Florissant are beautifully preserved, but frequently it is possible to observe damage that has been caused by insects. The presence of thickened reaction

above: Feeding between the veins by insects has damaged this leaf of *Paracarpinus fratorna* (Betulaceae: Birch family) from the Late Eocene of Florissant, Colorado, USA.

tissue around the wound enables us to be sure that this sort of damage we see was caused by insects rather than through post mortem decay or through the rigors of the fossilisation process. The formation of reaction tissue means that the leaf was still alive when the damage occurred. Because of the quality of the preservation at Florissant and the number of fossils available for study, it has been possible to make quantitative assessments of the effects of insect damage. One study has shown that 23 per cent of leaves show signs of insect attack, with 1.4 per cent of the total leaf area of all leaves removed. This is much less than in modern forests where 72–90 per cent of leaves have been damaged and 4–10 per cent of the leaf area removed. In general, one needs to interpret results of this nature cautiously because there are several possible ways in which our assessment of the extent of insect damage can be distorted. For example, if one bases one's analysis on museum collections, then one has to be aware of collector bias. Insect activity could be under-represented because the original collector valued complete leaves and discarded damaged ones. Problems of this nature can be addressed by making new collections.

One of the most familiar and economically important ways in which arthropods interact with plants is in the process of pollination. Plants entice insects to flowers by offering them a reward in the form of food such as nectar, oils, and pollen. A portion of the pollen is deposited on the insect so that it can hitch a ride to the next flower or individual. In this way plants can target their pollen more cost effectively than by simply casting it into the wind. Nowadays, insect pollination is associated predominantly with flowering plants, and pollinators are found in virtually all insect orders, but notably Coleoptera (beetles), Diptera (true flies), Lepidoptera (butterflies, moths), Thysanoptera (thrips), and Hymenoptera (bees, ants, wasps). Pollination is however a more general phenomenon in plants, and the association between plants and insect pollinators has a long history.

above: Bee preserved in amber, *Prolebeia dominicana*, 4 mm long (Miocene, the Dominican Republic).

Insect pollination is thought to have its origins in the seed ferns of the Carboniferous Period. There is evidence from the elaborate form of some of their pollen-bearing organs and the nature of the pollen itself that animal vectors were involved in the pollination of some extinct pteridosperms. This is also consistent with the frequent finding of fossil pollen in the faecal pellets, and more rarely the gut contents, of hemipteroid and orthopteroid insects of this age. Furthermore, insect pollination is known from or likely in other groups of living and extinct gymnosperms. Living cycads are pollinated by beetles or small bees, and some living gymnosperms in the Gnetales are known to be visited by nectar-feeding moths. During the Mesozoic, extinct plants such as the Bennettitales may also have been insect pollinated. The structure of the flower-like reproductive organ in Bennettitales (see Chapter 8) – in particular the great degree to which the ovules are hidden away and shielded – is consistent with pollination by insects with chewing mouthparts, such as the beetles. Both beetles and flies are known to have been prominent insects during the Mesozoic Era.

Flowering plants may also have relied on insect pollination from the outset. Fossils of this important modern plant group first appeared during the Cretaceous Period, and we will see in the next chapter that many of the earliest flowers had adaptations to insect pollination (Chapter 8). Several potential insect pollinating groups were already present by the Early Cretaceous. The beetles and flies were already diverse, and both groups could have been playing a role in the pollination of gymnosperms at that time. Micropterigid moths that resemble the pollinators of living *Zygogynum* (Winteraceae) are also known, as are early relatives of the bees, such as sawflies and sphecid wasps. The flowering plants have exploited insect pollinators like no other plant group, and it is to flowers and their origin that we turn to next.

Chapter Eight

MODERN EARTH –
THE RISE OF FLOWERS

FLOWERS ARE AMONG the most aesthetically pleasing of nature's creations, and the plants that produce them are some of the most useful organisms known to humans. The seemingly endless list of commodities developed from flowering plants includes wood, fibres, paper, plastics, oils, resins, waxes, foods, herbs and spices, fabrics, dyes, drugs and medicines. Underpinning their enormous economic value is an astonishing breadth of diversity. This is reflected both in the varied range of habitats they occupy and in the large number of living species. Conservative estimates place the figure at over 220,000 species worldwide, which represents more than 80 per cent of the known diversity of land-dwelling plants.

From a geological perspective flowering plants are comparative newcomers. Their rise has been recent and spectacular. The earliest unmistakable fossil comes from the latter part of the Mesozoic, but the group did not achieve ecological hegemony until the close of the Cretaceous. Throughout the Cenozoic, relentless speciation within flowering plants added to the total diversity of the world's flora on an unprecedented scale. The measure of this success is that flowers have replaced gymnosperms and ferns as the dominant groups in most habitats. Although many theories have been advanced to explain their rapid rise, the causes underlying the success of flowering plants are still very much a matter for research and debate.

left: Leaf of flowering plant, *Rhus stellariaefolia*, approximately 11 cm in length, from Florissant, Colorado, USA (Late Eocene).

AN ABOMINABLE MYSTERY

In a letter to the botanist Joseph Dalton Hooker dated 22 July 1879, Charles Darwin famously portrayed the rapid development of flowering plants within recent geological times as 'an abominable mystery'. By that he meant that the causes of the fundamental change from floras typified by ferns, conifers and the like to ones dominated by flowering plants were poorly understood. Many theories have been advanced to explain how flowering plants originated and subsequently diversified so rapidly, but none of these is entirely satisfactory. Today, over 125 years later, we know much more about the geological history of the group and their interrelationships. Many of the more outlandish theories can be ruled out, and much of the mystique surrounding the origins of the group has been lifted. Botanists are closing in on solutions to problems that they have struggled with for generations.

The origin of flowering plants is one of the most widely discussed and enduring mysteries in the history of life on Earth. This subject encompasses many questions related to place and time of origin, as well as such issues as whether or not the flower evolved independently in several lineages, how flowering plants are related to other plant groups, and the development and assembly through time of the elements of the flower, such as petals, sepals, ovaries, stamens, etc. One difficulty has been the lack of consensus about which, of one or more of a number of living families,

above: Large flowering shrubs and trees shed numerous leaves throughout their lifespans. These are comparatively common and easily recognised fossils in the latter part of the Cretaceous and throughout the Cenozoic. *Populus latior*, approximately 11 cm wide (Miocene of Oeningen, near Baden, Germany).

is actually the first branch of the flowering plant family tree. Because of this gap in our knowledge, what constitutes the primitive condition in such key features as the flower has been difficult to assess. A second problem relates to the fossil record. Although the rocks are replete with information on pollen, leaves, fruit and wood, the record of flowers is sparse. This means that one of the crucial features of flowering plants has remained poorly characterised in early members of the group. Also, most fossils represent organs or plant fragments rather than whole individuals. Their significance is therefore not always easily interpreted. A third problem relates to the group of organisms that gave rise to flowering plants. It is clear that the ancestors of flowers were organisms that we would now classify as gymnosperms, but there are conflicting ideas on which living or extinct groups of gymnosperms constitute the closest relatives. Furthermore, flowering plants have diverged substantially in a number of ways. This hinders comparisons between for example aspects of the flower and plausibly equivalent reproductive features of

gymnosperms. In other words, the very characteristics of flowering plants that make them distinctive and so unique in many ways serve also to obscure their relations to other types of plant.

THE FIRST FLOWERS

Flowers are rare fossils, and this scarcity is related to their fleeting lifespans and to the fact that they are made up of many parts, which tend to fragment with age. Gardeners know how showy blooms eventually fall apart, creating a cascade of individual parts, such as

above: Rare fossilised flower preserved as a thin film of carbon on the rock. *Porana oeningensis*, 2 cm wide, from the Miocene of Oeningen, Germany.

petals and stamens. The rigours of fossilisation usually entail further disruption to fragile organs through the processes of transportation and burial in sediment. So the nature of the flower itself and the process of fossilisation mean that on the whole flowers are underrepresented as fossils. Specimens that do survive intact are commonly preserved as compressions, that is the original tissues have been reduced to a thin film of carbon on the rock. Even though these can be quite informative about the overall arrangement of floral parts, there is seldom much information preserved on critical anatomical details, such as the structure of the ovary or the pollen and pollen sacs, and the preservation of the finer cellular structure of delicate tissue is rarer still. Yet, it is details such as these that hold the key to unravelling the mystery of the origins of flowers. Despite the abundance of fossilised leaves, wood, fruits, seeds and pollen, in rocks of the Cretaceous, until recently only two structurally preserved flowers were known. All this changed in 1981 when the Danish palaeobotanist Else Marie Friis and the Swedish palynologist Annie Skarby unearthed exquisitely preserved fossil flowers from a china clay pit in southern Sweden.

China clay is composed chiefly of the mineral kaolinite, which is commonly formed by the weathering and decomposition of rocks containing aluminium silicate compounds. During the Cretaceous, large deposits formed in Europe and North America, and today these are mined for a variety of industrial applications ranging from the manufacture of fine porcelains to the production of high quality paper. Unlike hard rocks, these clays when mixed with water turn into a slurry, which is one of the reasons that they are so useful. This property also enables microscopic fossils to be recovered easily, simply by dropping the clay into water followed by sieving the slurry mix. In this way, any entombed fossils are caught in the sieve mesh. It was while searching the clays for fossil pollen using this method that Annie Skarby came across small fragments of charcoal that looked like flowers. These were brought to the attention of Else Marie Friis – a specialist in the fossil record of flowering plants – who made a detailed study confirming that they were indeed minute flowers preserved in exquisite detail.

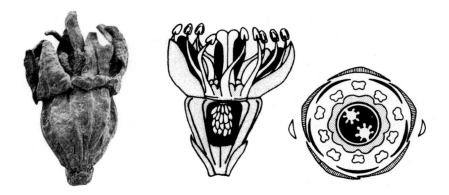

above left: Flower fossilised in charcoal: *Scandianthus costatus*, approximately 2 mm long, from the Upper Cretaceous of Åsen, Sweden. Image was made using a scanning electron microscope.
above right: Simplified diagram of the fossil flower *Scandianthus* from the Upper Cretaceous of Åsen, Sweden, with one sepal and part of the ovary wall removed to show the stigma, stamens and placenta (left). Plan view showing the arrangement of parts (right).

One of the first flowers to be described was named *Scandianthus*. At about 2 mm in length and 1 mm in breadth it is truly minute. The flower has been reduced to charcoal, and one of the remarkable consequences of this mode of fossilisation is that the organs and tissue systems are preserved in three dimensions, rather than as flattened compressions. The flowers had a regular radial symmetry, with parts in whorls. Sepals and petals numbered five. Each flower bore both male and female parts, and because of the preservation in charcoal these can be documented in some detail. We know that there were ten stamens, and that the anthers split lengthways to release tiny pollen grains. Also, it is possible to discern structures within the ovary, and possibly also a lobed nectary. Based on these data, Friis and Skarby concluded that the plant bearing these flowers was a member of the Saxifragaceae, a group that today includes saxifrages, hydrangeas and currants.

Since the description of *Scandianthus*, many fossilised flowers, fruits, and seeds have been sieved out of clay deposits from Europe and North America. These provide a completely new insight into the biology and diversity of flowering plants during the Cretaceous. Flowers discovered thus far are uniformly small, frequently less than 2 mm in length, and they are of simple unelaborated construction. Generally they are composed of few parts and the sepals and petals were uniform and similar to each other. The plants bearing these early flowers were probably herbaceous and of small stature rather than large and woody. These observations challenge hypotheses developed at the turn of the nineteenth century, which emphasised large multipart flowers such as those of *Magnolia* as a starting point in the evolution of flowers. If *Magnolia* is a poor model for the structure of early flowers, then what among the modern flora would be better suited? The close living relatives of modern magnolias actually exhibit a great variation in floral structure that also encompassed the small and simple. Some of the early flowers were probably closer in structure and relationship to groups such as the Piperales (Pepper, Kava), Chloranthaceae (*Chloranthus, Hedyosmum*), Lauraceae (Avocado, Bay Laurel, Cinnamon) and Calycanthaceae (Carolina Allspice, *Chimonanthus*).

The level of detail recoverable from flowers fossilised in charcoal also provides insights into their pollination biology. A series of tell-tale clues in the organs that contain the pollen implicate insects as vectors. The stamens had small anthers with low pollen output, and pollen was released through a flap of tissue known as a valve. The grains were frequently covered with pollenkitt, a sticky material that tended to hold them in clumps, and individual grains were smaller than the optimum size for dispersal via wind. Also, features resembling nectar-containing glands were noted in some species. These observations, together with the absence of an elaborate stigmatic surface crowning the carpel all suggest that many early flowering plants were insect-pollinated rather than wind-pollinated. Pollinators could have included beetles, flies and moths. Today, the Hymenoptera (bees, wasps and sawflies) are the most important pollinators of flowering plants. Early relatives of the bees, such as sawflies and sphecid wasps, may also have played a role in pollination of the earliest flowers. Even though early angiosperms may have been very similar to their living relatives in pollination syndrome, modes of fruit and seed dispersal were probably very different. Cretaceous fruits and seeds are generally very small compared to their modern relatives, and there is no

above: Wind-dispersed seed: *Acer pseudocampestre*, 3 cm long, from the Oligocene of Preschen, Bohemia, Czech Republic.

evidence of specialised mammal or bird dispersal. Among basal groups of angiosperms, the evolution of fleshy fruits, seeds with fleshy or hairy outgrowths, and other adaptations for animal dispersal seems to be correlated with the evolution of fruit and seed-eating birds and mammals, perhaps during the latest Cretaceous but most strikingly during the early part of the Cenozoic.

DISTANT COUSINS

Flowering plants are known to be close relatives of the gymnosperms, a group that includes such living forms as conifers and cycads as well as an enormous variety of extinct species. Of the many things that point to a close relationship, one of the most obvious is their reproductive biology. Plants in both groups reproduce by means of seeds, which are unique organs found nowhere else in the Plant Kingdom. This close kinship has recently been confirmed by a detailed comparison of gene sequences in the DNA of living species. These data show clearly that flowering plants had a single origin, but the precise identity of their closest relatives within the gymnosperms is still unclear.

When botanists say that flowering plants and gymnosperms are closely related they are talking in strictly relative terms. They mean that the flowering plants are closer to the gymnosperms than they are to any other group of plants. This does not necessarily mean that this relationship is a recent one. In fact, the fossil record tells us just the opposite. The split between the two is very ancient indeed. They are more like very distant cousins than brother and sister. Another issue is the degree to which these groups have changed in appearance through time. The flowering plants have developed their own unique qualities, many of which are embodied in the flower. Living gymnosperms do not have such things as petals and carpels, but they do have the equivalent of pollen and anthers. This means that the early ancestors of the flowering plants would have borne a much closer resemblance to their gymnosperm cousins. For the palaeobotanist in search of early fossil evidence this poses a problem. How does one recognise early relatives of the flowering plants, and how does one go about distinguishing them from other gymnosperms? One approach is to sift through gymnosperm-like fossils looking for species that share one or more of the unique features of flowering plants, but such things are often difficult to recognise.

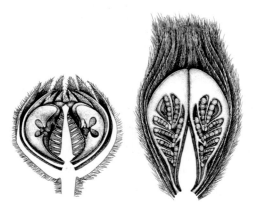

above: Flower-like organs are found in the extinct Bennettitales. Section through 'flower' of *Williamsoniella coronata* (left): ovules are borne on a central mound flanked by pollen-bearing organs and outer whorls of petal-like bracts. Section through 'flower' of *Cycadeoidea* (right): it is now thought unlikely that this complex pollen and ovule-bearing structure opened out like a flower.

Flower-like organs are known in some extinct gymnosperms. We have seen how the cycad-like Bennettitales were common in the Late Triassic through to the latter part of the Cretaceous. These plants bore flower-like organs positioned at the ends of stems or embedded among the bristle of leaf bases that covered the outer surface of the trunks. The ovules or female organs were enveloped by a 'perianth' of

above: The flowers of the early flowering plant *Archaefructus sinensis* did not bear petals and sepals, and experts differ in their interpretation over whether these were complex solitary flowers or inflorescences. Based on fossils from the Early Cretaceous of Beipiao and Lingyuan provinces, western Liaoning, China.

above: Thin stems, narrow branched leaves and associated fish are consistent with an aquatic habitat for the early flowering plant *Archaefructus sinensis*. From the Early Cretaceous of Beipiao and Lingyuan provinces, western Liaoning, China.

bracts resembling the petals or sepals of flowers. Technically these organs differed from true flowers because the ovules were not enclosed within a carpel. They were arrayed on a mound of tissue within the centre of the flower-like head. In 1916, George Reber Wieland, working at Yale, famously depicted the 'flower' of *Cycadeoidea* with a large showy perianth, but it is now thought unlikely that the bracts opened out in this way. The male organs of some Bennettitales and such obscure living gymnosperms as the Gnetales (e.g. *Ephedra*, *Welwitschia*) also share flower-like qualities. The 'anthers' were aggregated together into whorls or pseudowhorls to form cup-like 'flowers' that were quite distinct from the pollen cones of the conifers. Features such as those exhibited in the male flower in particular have been used to link groups such as Gnetales and Bennettitales to the flowering plants.

There are several extinct gymnosperms known from rocks of the Mesozoic that are good candidates for the closest relative of the flowering plants. One plant with excellent credentials is *Archaefructus liaoningensis* which comes from the Early Cretaceous Jehol Biota of north-east China. This series of sediments is famed for its animals, especially the extraordinary bird-like feathered dinosaurs. *Archaefructus* is thought to have been an herbaceous aquatic. It had thin stems and finely dissected compound leaves. The solitary 'flower' presents a unique combination of features. A stem-like central branch bore clusters of appendages interpreted as carpels. Below these was a zone of stamens. The pollen – although not well-preserved – resembled that of other flowering plants commonly found dispersed in Cretaceous sediments. Unlike most modern species though, the 'flower' of *Archaefructus* did not have petals and sepals. On the face of it, this intriguing fossil would seem to present a set of features that are intermediate between true flowering plants and other gymnosperms.

The interpretation of fossil plants is seldom straightforward, and *Archaefructus* raises almost as many questions as it answers. One problem is that some important details such as the anatomy of the carpels and the anthers remain by and large unknown. This introduces a degree of ambiguity in our estimation of where *Archaefructus* sits in relation to other gymnosperms and to the flowering plants. Furthermore, experts differ in their interpretation of the flower. Some regard this not as a complex solitary flower, but more like an inflorescence. In other words, it is conceivable that the individual male and female elements are each flowers in their own right. Under this interpretation, individual flowers still do not possess petals or sepals, just the bare bones of their female or male sexual identity.

Another possibility is that *Archaefructus* is in fact a fully-fledged flowering plant with a very atypical inflorescence. Living species that flower underwater often no longer have petals and sepals. In the underwater environment these are redundant parts, so over time they have been lost in some aquatic species. Perhaps the absence of petals and sepals in *Archaefructus* is a derived rather than a primitive feature. Could *Archaefructus* simply be a bizarre aquatic flowering plant? The answers to questions like these lie buried in the details of the anatomy of the floral organs and await further discoveries among the fossilised remains of the plants of the Mesozoic.

TIME AND PLACE

Establishing the time and place of origin of a group of organisms is apt to be a slippery business. First, one must recognise that taxonomic groups can be defined in subtly different ways. Unfortunately, this can result in one name being used to circumscribe similar (but slightly more or less inclusive) groups by different scientists. One needs therefore to be clear about the definitions used. Second, our knowledge of what constitutes a member of a group of organisms also changes as scientists make further discoveries. This is an inevitable consequence of the scientific process. Third, many fossil plants represent only small parts of a whole organism, so the degree to which we can be confident about assigning them to a group varies, and may itself be the subject of controversy within the scientific community. To further muddy the waters, each group of organisms can be thought of as having two starting points; the first being the point at which its lineage splits from others (total group) and the second being the point to which all living species can trace their most recent common ancestor (crown group). These rather technical considerations are important because misunderstandings here can lead to confusion. Members of the so-called crown group contain all of the attributes that we associate with modern flowering plants, whereas members of the total group do not. They may be deficient in one or more respects. There can also be a huge time interval between the origin of the total group and the origin of the crown group, as appears to be the case with the flowering plants.

It is clear from an examination of the fossil record that the Cretaceous holds the key to understanding much of the early evolution of the flowering plants. It is during the Cretaceous that the first unmistakable fossils appear. The most abundant evidence comes in the form of microscopic grains of pollen. In certain groups the pollen has distinctive attributes, and when we observe grains like these in a fossilised state we know that we have evidence of the presence of flowering plants. More than 75 per cent of living species belong to a group called eudicots, and these typically possess pollen grains bearing three elongate furrows or forms that are likely derived from this type. This so-called triaperturate pollen is first documented in sediments that are about 125 million years old. Earlier still in the Cretaceous are pollen grains called *Clavatipollenites*. These possess a single furrow, which is a feature shared by some gymnosperms and by some flowering plants. These grains are however believed to have been shed by *bona fide* flowering plants because of certain details of the structure of the pollen cell wall. *Clavatipollenites* resembles pollen found today in plants related to the chloranthoids and the Piperales. The evidence from the pollen corroborates data from other sources, in particular fossil leaves, pointing to a Cretaceous origin and diversification of the flowering plant crown group.

Pollen can be so ubiquitous in sedimentary rocks deposited on or near continents that it provides perhaps the most complete record of changes in plant life through time. By measuring the abundance of certain pollen types and by counting the number of different forms scientists are able to build up a picture of floral change through geological time. During the late 1980s, Peter R Crane and Scott Lidgard of Chicago's Field Museum decided to explore the question of the time and place of flowering plant origins by looking in detail at the pollen evidence. Their approach was to quantify aspects of pollen diversity for different latitudes through the Cretaceous of the Northern Hemisphere. By latitudes they meant the palaeolatitude or the latitude of a site in the past, taking into account the effects of continental drift. In this way they were able to plot (by latitude) the spread of flowering plants through the Cretaceous. Their results showed that flowering plants first appeared at low latitudes, ones that would nowadays be in the tropics, and that the group moved polewards thereafter. Throughout the Cretaceous the diversity was always lower at high latitude than at corresponding low latitudes. In summary, the results showed that the burgeoning of the flowering plant crown group began at low latitudes and moved progressively northwards. These observations furnish a new set of clues to the reasons that might underlie the early success of the group. One of these may have been ecological. Geological evidence indicates that at the time, low latitudes were prone to seasonal aridity. Such environments might have favoured flowering plants with short-lived weedy life histories. This is one reproductive strategy that could have contributed to the high speciation rates necessary to sustain the rapid diversification of the group.

If the Cretaceous witnessed the rise to prominence of the flowering plants, when did the group originate? Or, to put it another way, when did the lineage leading to the flowering plants split off from its nearest living relatives in the gymnosperms? This is much more controversial, because the precise identity of the nearest living relative of the flowering plants is still debated. Two principal hypotheses have been advocated recently, and each has different implications for the genesis of the group. One hypothesis views living gymnosperms in the Gnetales as the closest living relatives. Also allied with the flowering plants are extinct forms such as the Bennettitales. Because pollen grains of probable gnetalean origin are known in rocks from the early part of the Triassic, one corollary of this hypothesis is that the lineage leading to flowering plants must have split off over 230 million years ago. A second widely advocated hypothesis suggests that

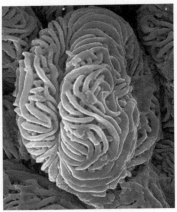

top: Pollen with one elongate slit *Clavatipollenites*-type has been observed attached to the stigma of early fossil flowers. (Measures approximately 20 μm in diameter).
above: Triaperturate pollen with three elongate slits or apertures (two visible and one hidden on the back side of the pollen grain). Forms derived from this are typical of most living flowering plants. (Measures approximately 20 μm in diameter).

flowering plants had an altogether more ancient origin. Recent comparisons of the gene sequences in the DNA of living species indicate that Gnetales might not be so closely related. Rather, the split happened further down the family tree. This would imply a still more ancient origin, perhaps in the latter part of the Carboniferous, over 290 million years ago. In either case, the lineage leading to the flowering plants is expected to have a long history pre-dating the Cretaceous.

In the view of flowering plant evolution outlined above, the genesis of the group precedes the appearance of unmistakable fossils by 100 million years or more. Furthermore, the ancient root of flowers is confirmed by analyses of gene sequences from living species. Nowadays, one can estimate the timing of the divergence of different lineages based on the degree of difference between comparable sequences of their DNA. This approach – the so-called 'molecular clock' – places the origin of flowering plants consistently earlier than does the fossil evidence, pushing them back in time towards the base of the Mesozoic or the latter part of the Palaeozoic. One is therefore justified in asking if there is any evidence for flowering plants that pre-dates the Cretaceous, and if not how do we explain the lengthy geological hiatus that seems to separate their genesis from the point at which they leave their mark upon the fossil record?

The scientific literature is replete with alleged flowering plant fossils from sediments that predate the Cretaceous. However, critical analysis by experts raises questions in all cases. Most of these supposed early flowers can be

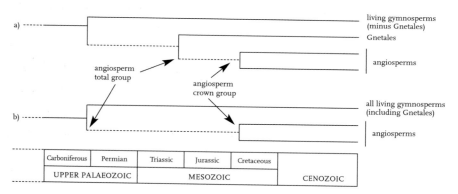

above: Two hypotheses that have very different implications for dating the split between flowering plants and other plant groups. Known geological ranges of groups indicated by solid lines; implied geological ranges indicated by broken lines.

shown to be misplaced stratigraphically (i.e. younger than supposed). Others were later discovered to be unrelated to flowering plants, or lacking the critical diagnostic features, or too poorly preserved to enable reliable identification. For example, pollen that resembles that of flowering plants is widely reported from sediments of Triassic and Jurassic age. The so-called Crinopolles group (Late Triassic) has a single furrow running lengthways and a reticulate pattern to the exterior wall that bears a strong resemblance to the pollen of some flowering plants. However, some of these features are also observed in gymnosperms, and on closer examination other features are seen to differ in significant ways from those in true flowering plants. So, although Crinopolles pollen grains might belong to extinct relatives of the flowering plants it is also possible that they might not. At the end of the day, the evidence is still equivocal. This highlights some of the difficulties of accurately attributing fossilised plant parts such as individual organs or organ systems to families or higher taxonomic groups.

Paradoxically, the lack of unmistakable fossil evidence in rocks that pre-date the Cretaceous is not itself inconsistent with an ancient origin of the lineage leading to the flowering plants. The diversification of the group during the Cretaceous is most likely a phenomenon of the crown group. By this we mean that it is during this time that the most ancient surviving modern lineages began to diverge. These organisms bore most or all of the hallmarks of living flowering plants, including true flowers. They are therefore recognisably distinct in many features from the gymnosperms, so they appear to us as an easily separable component of fossil floras. Earlier, in the pre-Cretaceous world, the ancestors of the flowering plants would have lacked one or more of the attributes that we associate with modern members of the group. Such distinctive features as the flower had not yet evolved, and the early relatives of the flowering plants would have resembled more closely their gymnosperm cousins. These plants would have blended into the background of shrubby Mesozoic gymnosperms, hidden among the conifers, cycads and their allies. The true affinity of many extinct Mesozoic gymnosperms may therefore lie closer to flowering plants than previously supposed.

MODERN FAMILIES

Of the many advances in recent years in our understanding of the origins of flowering plants, one of the most important comes, not from the fossil record, but from the comparative study of the systematics of living species. By comparing aspects of the structure of DNA from different living organisms it is possible to begin for the first time to uncover the history of flowering plants through knowledge of their family tree. This approach is now shedding light on a problem that has plagued botanists for over 100 years. How are the 350 to 400 or so living families of flowering plants actually related to each other? The reason that this is important is that it allows us to identify those species that are on the early branches of the tree, which enables us to build up a picture of what the early flowering plants might have looked like. Also, by knowing more about when various families make their appearance in relation to each other we can obtain clues on what we might expect to find among the fossils. Studying the relationships of living species can therefore inform the palaeobotanist on many levels.

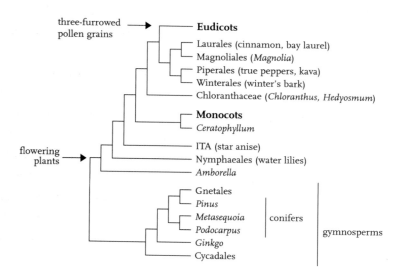

above: The basal branches of the flowering plant family tree as discovered from gene sequences.

Research of this nature has confirmed that the earliest branches of the flowering plant family tree lie within the magnoliid dicotyledons. This small group of families makes up about 3 per cent of the living species diversity, and it includes familiar forms such as the Nymphaeales (water lilies), Piperales (true peppers), Magnoliaceae (magnolias) and a handful of other related types such as Winteraceae (Winter's Bark), Chloranthaceae (*Chloranthus, Sarcandra, Hedyosmum*), and Lauraceae (Avocado, Bay Laurel, Cinnamon). Detailed comparisons of gene sequences have identified the water lilies together with four other small groups (Amborellaceae, Illiciales, Trimeniaceae, Austrobaileyaceae) as the first living lineages to diverge. From within this miscellaneous assemblage emerge two other major players. These are the monocotyledons and the eudicots. The monocotyledons comprise 22 per cent of living species diversity, including plants such as orchids, grasses and palms. The eudicots contains the vast majority of flowering plants, over 75 per cent of the living species. Based on our knowledge of the relationships among these groups, we would expect to be able to place early fossils in or close to one or more of the families of magnoliid dicotyledons. We would also expect to unearth fossils exhibiting similarities to primitive eudicots and monocotyledons.

Even though the oldest fossilised flowers and fruits are rarely assignable to living families or orders, they do show a blend of features of the general magnoliid type. Also, some fossils appear to combine the characteristics of more than one living family. These observations imply that the flowering plant crown group was well established by at least 136 million years ago. Beginning about 127 million years ago, we see fossils with recognisable affinities to modern families. These include the fruits, seeds, flowers and pollen of plants related to water

above: Relatives of the water lilies were among the earliest flowering plants. Flower is approximately 2 mm wide (Early Cretaceous, Portugal).

lilies (Nymphaeaceae), Chloranthaceae, Lauraceae, Winteraceae, Magnoliales, and possibly Piperales. By 112 million years ago it is clear that the magnoliid dicotyledons had diversified into a number of lineages. One surprising aspect of the fossil record at this time is the dearth of evidence for the monocotyledons. The family tree of flowers predicts that the monocotyledons should emerge at about the same time as the magnoliid dicotyledons are diversifying. Their absence from early floras is a puzzle, but it may prove to be more apparent than real. Perhaps it reflects a representation bias. Monocotyledons might not have been abundant initially near areas of fossilisation, or perhaps being less woody than the magnoliid dicotyledons they were not preserved in as great a number. Another possibility is that we are unable to recognise monocotyledons because they were not yet distinctive enough from their close relatives in the magnoliid dicotyledons. Whatever the reason, the monocotyledons are clearly represented in later fossil assemblages from the Late Cretaceous. The earliest unmistakable fossils include fruits of the ginger family (Zingiberales) and the leaves and stems of palms (Arecales). Other important groups such as grasses did not become abundant and widespread until much more recently, during the latter part of the Oligocene and Miocene, 28–10 million years ago. Others, although undoubtedly ancient, have left no fossil footprint, for example, the orchids have no fossil record to speak of. The reason for this is most likely related to the places in which orchids grow.

The fossilised remains of three furrowed pollen grains signal the early development of the eudicots. These begin to turn up in numbers in 127 million-year-old sediments. The origin of eudicots was therefore an early event, as predicted in the family tree of flowers. From about 112 million years ago fossils related to modern groups such as the Plane and Buttonwood trees (Platanaceae) and probably also the Box family (Buxaceae) are recognisable. The number of living families represented as fossils increased progressively through the latter part of the Cretaceous. By about 93 million years ago, we had plants related to the Witch Hazels and Sweet Gums (Hamamelidaceae) and the Saxifrages (Saxifragales). The rosids also first

appeared at about this time. There is evidence for the
Capers (Capparales) and somewhat later records of
the Myrtales, Walnuts, Hickories and Pecan Nuts
group (Juglandales), Myricales, and the Birches,
Alders, Beeches and Oaks group (Fagales). The
main asterid lineage was also present and
represented by flowers of ericalean affinity,
and members of the Hydrangeaceae have
been recorded at about the same time. Nearly
all of the main groups of eudicots are represented
by at least one member of their lineage in the Late
Cretaceous. There are however some notable
exceptions. These include the Pea or the Bean family
(Fabaceae), the Sunflower family (Asteraceae), the Lamiales
and the Gentianales; which together comprise 45
per cent of living species diversity in eudicots.
The three subfamilies of Pea are well
documented by flowers and fruits in the Eocene,
and there is some evidence from pollen grains

above: The pea family are comparative latecomers. Part of *Acacia*-like pod, 14 cm long, from the Eocene of the Paris Basin.

that the range of the group might have extended back into the latest part of
the Cretaceous. The earliest unequivocal records of the Asteraceae, Lamiales
and Gentianales come from the Paleogene. The fact that most species rich
groups are known from relatively young fossils indicates that a significant
proportion of eudicot diversity is the product of radiations that occurred
during the latter half of flowering plant evolution. The evolutionary basis for
the rapid diversification of specific eudicot groups remains largely unknown.

By the end of the Cretaceous about 50–80 per cent of land plant species
were flowering plants, and this group was the dominant vegetation over
large tracts of land, particularly at low latitudes. On a geological scale, their
rapid rise to prominence is still regarded as unprecedented, and their effects
on the world's flora have been profound and long lasting. Modern science has
fleshed out many of the details of Darwin's abominable mystery. The marvels

of gene sequencing have enabled us to reconstruct the broad outlines of the family tree of flowers. The wonders of the fossil record have faithfully preserved for over 100 million years the minute details of tiny flowers. And, on an even smaller but vastly more numerous scale, microscopic fossil pollen grains reflect changes in vegetation patterns at a global level. Yet, despite these advances and new perspectives, many questions still remain unanswered. Of these, perhaps the most elusive concern the causes driving the success of flowering plants. Why flowers, and why are there so many species? These are questions that we are still a long way from answering.

SUMMATION
· · · · · · · · · · · · · · · · · ·

NATURAL CURIOSITY COMPELS us to ask questions about the world and to speculate on the origin and meaning of such things as fossils. This inquisitiveness is shaped by our worldviews, and the answers that we seek have varied across cultures and through time. Thus, to the Navaho Indians of North America the petrified logs of the famous fossil forest in Arizona were the bones of a monster whose congealed blood is to be seen in adjacent lava flows. In nineteenth century Europe, natural historians wrote books on how to reconcile the testimony of the rocks with the account of a great flood written in the Judeo-Christian scriptures (Genesis). Elsewhere, fossil wood has been imbued with mystical significance, and it is occasionally encountered in burial chambers or places of worship. Modern science has dropped the mythological and theological in favour of explanations couched in terms of natural causes. This approach is called methodological naturalism, and its results have achieved an unprecedented degree of corroboration and acceptance across cultural divides. The collection, study, and interpretation of fossils over the past 200 years have changed our view of the world and the sense that we have of our relationship with nature.

One reason therefore to study fossil plants is the fascination that we hold for things historical. We desire to know something of the past. We have a natural inclination to wonder about our origins. We are also motivated by the thrill of exploration and discovery. The prospect of travelling back in time cannot be realised, but the fossil record affords a kind of window onto the past, a form of surrogate time travel. The unearthing of a once-living organism that has lain buried in the rocks for hundreds of millions of years is to touch a piece of history for the first time. For many palaeontologists such feelings and experiences are the nurseries of our professional ambitions.

As one learns more about fossil plants, so the intellectual challenges begin to emerge and the role that palaeobotany plays in the broader scheme of scientific endeavour starts to take shape. There is the narrative dimension. What happened and when? The chronology of events and the documentation of the evolution of plants are key functions of palaeobotany. These are essentially open-ended domains of research. They have no definite end point where we can say that we know all that there is to know about the flora of a particular region or age. There are many areas of the world where even very basic surveys of the fossil floras have yet to be undertaken. This sort of work adds to the great body of knowledge on the history of plant life, and it often throws up interesting new discoveries. Thus, recording the kinds of fossil plants that occur at a particular place during a particular time allows us to map changes in plant life through the ages. Research of this nature forms the fundamental empirical framework that underpins much of our knowledge of the evolution of plants and the environments in which they lived.

Of the great lessons that humankind has learned from palaeontology, there are at least two that have far reaching implications for the future. These are to do with the causes of extinction and the effects of climate change. We know for sure that the nature of the world's flora has changed down the ages. We know that extinction has cut a great swathe through this green web of life, but we still have much to learn about its causes. Why is extinction much more widespread during certain intervals of geological time? What are the roles of climate change and natural catastrophes? There is also much to learn about how different groups of organisms have responded to their environments. Plants differ from animals in so many ways, not least in their sedentary mode of life, their very dissimilar reproductive biology, and their ability to regenerate following catastrophic organ and tissue loss. Closely linked to the issue of extinction is the nature of climate change on a global scale, an area in which palaeobotany has much to contribute. Plants are sensitive to the climatic regimes under which they grow. Many aspects of their form are fine-tuned to temperature, light, and water availability. Furthermore, variations in these parameters are faithfully recorded in tissues as they grow. The fossil record of plants contributes to our understanding of the nature and scale of environmental change through geological time. Knowing this bigger picture is essential to gauging the effects of changing climates on the shorter historical timescales that influence human societies.

Because of the ravages of extinction much of what we are likely to learn about the evolution of plants still lies buried in the rocks. Fossils help us to plug huge gaps in our knowledge of plant diversity that is simply not recoverable from a study of living species alone. One area of current scientific endeavour is the piecing together of the Tree of Life. The challenge here is to discover the tree or network that best specifies the relationships among living organisms ranging from bacteria to humans. This is a vast undertaking that involves numerous scientists around the world. Fossil plants are useful not only because they fill in gaps caused by extinction but because they enable that limb of the Tree of Life dealing with plants to be dated with reference to the geological timescale. Another area of major scientific endeavour is the investigation of how genes act in concert to create the organs and the tissue systems of plants. The sort of information that can be gleaned from fossils can usefully be applied to the investigation of the development of important organ systems such as leaves, seeds, wood, roots, etc. In the not so distant future it will be possible to test ideas developed using fossils against theories worked out from laboratory studies of how genes interact in living species to produce the vast diversity of organ systems that we see today.

Plants were among the earliest organisms to adapt successfully to life on land. We have seen how the earliest forms were tiny and almost unrecognisable to the modern eye. The legacy of their green algal ancestors was by and large limited to the machinery of the cell, which for over 400 million years has proven to be a remarkably proficient and adaptable biochemical powerhouse. Like no other group of organisms, the shape and form of plants and their biology has been fashioned by their interactions with the gaseous medium of the atmosphere. That is not to underplay the influence that plants have had on each other or their numerous interactions with animals. It is simply recognition of the overwhelming importance that physical aspects of the environment have had on the evolution of this group. Plants have colonised, exploited and adapted to all but the most arid and cold environments. The relentless advance of this vegetation has been shaped by and given shape to the landscape, and where plants have led animals of one sort or another have followed. It is the fundamental role that plants play at the base of the terrestrial ecosystem that makes them such important and fascinating subjects of study. They are also the world's most silent, immobile, resilient and ubiquitous witnesses to the passage of time.

Further Information

Coal: its origin and future, A.C. Scott. Teaching Earth Sciences, 16: 24-36, 1991.

Cradle of life: the discovery of Earth's earliest fossils, W.J. Schopf. Princeton University Press, Princeton, New Jersey, 367 pp., 1999.

Extinctions in the history of life, P.D. Taylor (Ed.) Cambridge University Press, Cambridge, 191 pp., 2004.

Food of the dinosaurs, B.A. Thomas and C.J. Cleal. National Museums & Galleries of Wales, Cardiff, 32 pp., 1998.

Fossil plants and spores: modern techniques, T.P. Jones and N.P. Rowe (Eds.) The Geological Society, London, 396 pp., 1999.

Palaeobiology II, D.E.G. Briggs and P.R. Crowther. Blackwell Science, Malden, MA, 583 pp., 2001

Paleobotany and the evolution of plants, W.N. Stewart and G.W. Rothwell. Cambridge University Press, Cambridge, 521 pp., 1993.

Petrified wood: the world of fossilized wood, cones, ferns, and cycads, F.J. Daniels. Western Colorado Pub. Co., Grand Junction, Colorado, 170 pp., 1988.

Plant-animal interactions: an evolutionary approach, C.M. Herrera and O. Pellmyr 2001. Blackwell Science, Oxford, 313 pp., 2001.

Reading the rocks: animals and plants in prehistoric Australia and New Zealand, M.E. White. Kangaroo Press, Sydney, 256 pp., 1999.

The biology and evolution of fossil plants, T.N.Taylor and E.L.Taylor. Prentice Hall, New Jersey, 982 pp., 1993.

The evolutionary biology of plants, K.J. Niklas. University of Chicago Press, Chicago, 449 pp., 1997.

The evolution of plants, K.J. Willis and J.C. McElwain. Oxford University Press, Oxford, 378 pp., 2002.

The origin of angiosperms and their biological consequences, E.M. Friis, W.G. Chaloner and P.R. Crane (Eds.). Cambridge University Press, Cambridge, 358 pp., 1987.

Glossary

Anther Part of a flower: the pollen-producing sacs (usually group of four) at the end of the stamen.

Arborescent Resembling a tree in form and branching structure.

Bennettitales An extinct order of Mesozoic gymnosperms resembling living cycads in habit and leaf shape.

Blue-green algae See cyanobacteria.

Bract Modified leaf or leaf-like part just below and protecting the inflorescence.

Bryophyte Usually small land plant belonging to one of three living groups known as liverworts, hornworts, and mosses.

Cambium Formative layer of tissue one cell thick between xylem and phloem in many vascular plants that is responsible for increase in girth of stems and trunks.

Carpel Part of a flower: the female ovule-bearing part composed of ovary, style and stigma.

Charophycean algae Closest living algal relatives of land plants. Small group comprising large complex types such as *Chara* and simpler filamentous forms like *Spirogyra*. Also known as a Charophyte.

Chert A hard sedimentary rock composed of fine-grained silica.

Chloroplast Microscopic subcellular structure that is the site of photosynthesis in plants and other eukaryotes.

Clubmosses An ancient plant group with few living species but many extinct forms – especially diverse during the Carboniferous Period. Clubmoss here is used to include plants in the living families Lycopodiaceae (clubmosses), Selaginellaceae (spikemosses), and Isoetaceae (quillworts), as well as the many extinct forms. Also known as lycopods, lycophytes, or lycopsids.

Conifer The largest and most widely distributed group of living gymnosperms. There are about 600 living species organised into ten families. Living species are predominantly shrubs or small trees with well-developed wood and needle-like or scale-like leaves. Included in this group are such common forms as pines and cypresses.

Cupule A cup-shaped structure bearing seeds.

Cuticle Waxy covering produced by the epidermal cells of leaves and stems to protect the plant from excessive water loss. Cuticle can become fossilised and it is able to retain an imprint of the underlying epidermal cell pattern.

Cyanobacteria Microscopic and predominantly photosynthetic prokaryotes containing a blue pigment in addition to chlorophyll. These organisms are the closest relatives of plant chloroplasts. Also known as blue-green algae.

Cycad Tropical to subtropical group of living gymnosperms. There are some 130 living species that are classified into four families. Typically, cycads have a palm-like or fern-like habit.

Cycadophyte Plants resembling cycads, including living cycads and extinct Bennettitales. It is now thought that these two groups are only distant relatives and that cycadophytes is not a natural group.

Dicotyledon A long recognised group of flowering plants that is no longer considered natural. Essentially, it comprises all flowering plants except the monocotyledons.

Epicontinental On the edges of continents, especially of shallow seas.

Epidermis The outermost cells of the plant body, usually a layer one cell thick.

Epiphyte Plant that derives moisture and nutrients from the air and rain. Epiphytes usually grow on other plants but they are not parasitic.

Eukaryote Organism comprising a cell or cells containing a membrane-bound nucleus. Most eukaryotes also possess several other subcellular packages or organelles including the mitochondrion and one or more types of plastid (e.g. chloroplasts), which have specific biochemical functions. All plants and animals are eukaryotes.

Fern An ancient group of plants typified by large feather-like leaves. There are over 12,000 living species arrayed in some 33 families. Also called Filicales.

Flora An assemblage of fossil plants from one site or age.

Flowering plant A massive group of plants conservatively estimated at over 220,000 living species classified into between 320 and 590 families. Nowadays this group accounts for most land plant diversity. Members are characterised by the possession of flowers that bear ovules (seeds) formed within a carpel.

Fusain Fossil charcoal, probably resulting from the combustion of plant material in naturally occurring wildfire.

Gnetales A distinctive order of gymnosperms comprising some 80 living species in the genera *Ephedra*, *Gnetum*, and *Welwitschia*.

Gondwana A super-continent situated in the Southern Hemisphere that contained South America, Africa, Madagascar, India, Australia, New Zealand, parts of Indonesia, and Antarctica.

Green algae A diverse group of green-pigmented algae with marine, freshwater, and terrestrial species.

Gymnosperms An ancient group of seed-bearing plants that comprises over 800 living species as well as many extinct forms. Unlike flowering plants, the seeds are not enclosed within a carpel. Members include conifers, cycads, *Ginkgo* and Gnetales.

Horsetails A small, highly distinctive, and ancient group containing some 18 living species. All living species are herbaceous and have jointed stems bearing whorls of narrow branches with tiny scale-like leaves.

Inflorescence A group or cluster of flowers on a branch.

Laurasia The name given to the Northern Hemisphere supercontinent consisting of North America, Europe, and much of Asia north of the Himalayas.

Lycophyte, Lycopod, Lycopsid See clubmosses.

Megaspore In plants with spores of two sizes, the larger kind of spore is called a megaspore; it usually germinates into the female (egg-producing) part of the life cycle.

Metamorphism A geological process that alters the original composition and texture of a rock through heat and pressure deep within the Earth's crust.

Microspore In plants with spores of two sizes, the smaller kind of spore is called a microspore; it usually germinates into the male (sperm-producing) part of the life cycle. Contrast with megaspore.

Monocotyledons A major group of flowering plants with some 65,000 living species. Almost half of these are either orchids or grasses, but the group also includes palms, bromeliads, aroids, and lilies.

Nectary Part of a flower: a sugar-secreting gland, often located at the base of a flower.

Ovary Part of a flower: the swollen basal part of the carpel, which contains the ovules.

Ovule In seed plants, the female gamete and its protective and nutritive tissue, which develops into the dispersal unit or seed after fertilisation.

Pangea The name given to an ancient supercontient comprising all land masses of the Earth, including Laurasia and Gondwana.

Perianth Part of a flower: collective term for the outer parts of a flower, consisting of the petals and sepals.

Petal Part of a flower: the inner part of the perianth. Often brightly coloured.

Petrifaction During fossilisation, infiltration of plant with minerals that preserve the form and structure of the original tissues.

Phloem Vascular tissue whose principal function is the transport of sugars and other substances produced by the plant. Phloem cells are living when functional, forming an interconnected system of cytoplasm.

Pinna One of many first order leaflets in a compound leaf.

Pinnule One of many second order leaflets in a compound leaf.

Progymnosperm An extinct group of plants with woody stems like gymnosperms but fern-like reproduction (e.g. *Archaeopteris*)

Pteridophyte A collective term used to encompass plants belonging to the fern, horsetail, and clubmoss groups.

Pteridosperm See Seed fern.

Pyrite An iron sulphide mineral (FeS_2) and common petrifying agent in fossil plants. Also known as Fool's Gold and Iron Pyrite.

Rhizome A horizontal plant stem bearing upright shoots and typically downward growing roots.

Seed The structure that develops from the fertilised ovule of gymnosperms and flowering plants.

Seed fern An extinct group of seed producing plants with fern-like foliage.

Seed plant A plant that reproduces by means of seeds. The group includes all gymnosperms and flowering plants as well as numerous extinct seed-producing forms.

Sepal Part of a flower: the outer part of the perianth. Usually green.

Sporangium (pl. sporangia) Tiny organs in which spores form.

Spore Microscopic usually single-celled reproductive body. Often airborne.

Sporophyll A modified leaf that bears sporangia.

Stamen Part of a flower: the male reproductive part comprising the anther, which is usually borne on a narrow stalk.

Stomatum (pl. stomata) Opening in the epidermis of a stem or leaf permitting gas exchange with the air. Each opening is formed and regulated by a pair of sausage-shaped guard cells.

Strobilus (pl. Strobili) A well-defined zone of closely packed spore-bearing leaves.

Stromatolite A layered, fossilised deposit, mainly of limestone, formed by photosynthesising colonial cyanobacteria and other microbes.

Subduction A large-scale geological process in which one edge of a crustal plate is forced downward into the mantle below another plate.

Tracheid A type of water-conducting xylem cell that is thickened and hardened by lignin.

Vascular system The continuous water and solute (sap) transport network comprising cells of the xylem and phloem.

Wood A tissue system comprising mainly cells of the xylem and fibres.

Xylem Vascular tissue whose principal function is the upward transport of water and solutes. Xylem cells are dead when functional, forming an interconnected system of hollow tubes.

Index

Picture Credits

p.12 © P. Kenrick; p.15 © J.W. Schopf; p.20 © Linda Graham; p.21 © Charles Wellman; p.22 (l) *Nature*, 357:683-685, Edwards, Davies & Axe, 1992, © Macmillan Publishers Ltd, (r) © P. Kenrick/Pollyanna von Knorring; p.25 Philip Rye/© NHM; p.26 (r) © P. Kenrick; p.27 © Jason Dunlop; p.36 © P. Kenrick; p.37 *Botanical Journal of the Linnean Society*, 61:37-64, Andrews & Phillips, 1968, © Linnean Society of London; p.39 © Prof Patricia Gensel; p.40 (t) *Palaeobotany and Evolution of Plants*, Stewart & Rothwell, 1993, Cambridge University Press, redrawn from *Canadian Journal of Botany*, 58:2241-62, Doran, 1980, National Research Council of Canada, (b) amended from *Nature*, 410:309-310, Kenrick, 2001, © Macmillan Publishers Ltd; p.43 *Palaeobotany and Evolution of Plants*, Stewart & Rothwell, 1993, Cambridge University Press, redrawn from *American Journal of Botany*, 49:373-382, Beck, 1968, Botanical Society of America; p.45 (l) *International Journal of Plant Sciences*, 153(4):602-621, Serbet & Rothwell, 1992, © University of Chicago Press, (r) *Palaeobotany and Evolution of Plants*, Stewart & Rothwell, 1993, Cambridge University Press, redrawn from *Contributions from the Museum of Paleontology*, University of Michigan, 22:139-154, Pettitt & Beck, 1968; pp.48-49 © P. Kenrick; p.51 Redrawn by Philip Rye from *Plants Invade the Land: Evolutionary and Environmental Consequences*, 218, Algeo, Scheckler & Maynard, 2001, © Columbia University Press; p.54 Redrawn by Philip Rye from *Palaeontology*, 43:1, Ash & Creber by permission of The Palaeontological Association; p.56 © Prof Andrew Scott; p.57 The Royal Collection © 2004, Her Majesty Queen Elizabeth II; p.59 © Ben A. LePage; p.60 © John L. Howard; p.62, p.63 (b) © P.G. Davis; p.65 © Glasgow Museums: Fossil Grove; p.66 © *Bulletin* 251, Plate 3, printed with permission of the New York State Museum, Albany, NY USA 12230; p.67 © Kleine Senckenberg-Reihe, 18, Schweitzer, Hans-Joachim, *Pflanzen erobern das Land*, 1990; p.69 Mike Eaton/© NHM; p.82 Redrawn by Lisa Wilson from *Atlas of Lithological Indicators of Climate*, A.J. Boucot, C. Xu, C.R. Scotese, SEPM; p.84 © The Field Museum GEO85637c; p.85, p.88 (l), p.91 (l), p.92 (l) Philip Rye/© NHM; p.93 *Botanical Gazette*, 145:275-291, Rothwell & Warner, 1984, © University of Chicago Press; p.98 © Dr J.C. Vogel; p.100 (bl) © P. Kenrick; p.101 (t) © P.D. Taylor; p.101 (b) © Prof R.A. Spicer; p.112 (t) © Scott Zona; p. 125 Amended from *Nature*, 399(6735):429-436, Petit *et al.*, 1999, © Macmillan Publishers Ltd; pp.132-133 © Jane Francis; p.138 © John Sibbick/NHMPL; p.140 Amended from *The Evolutionary Biology of Plants*, Niklas, 1997, © University of Chicago Press; p.142 © Jane Francis; p.156 *Palaeobotany and Evolution of Plants*, Stewart & Rothwell, 1993, Cambridge University Press, redrawn from *Alcheringa*, 1:387-399, Gould & Delevoryas, 1977, Geological Society of Australia; p.158 Perks Willis Design/© NHM; p.164 *Review of Palaeobotany and Palynology*, vol.90, D. Edwards *et al.*, New insights into early land ecosystems, 1996, © Elsevier; p.168 © Michael Long/NHMPL; p.172 Philip Rye/© NHM; pp.173-174 © Zhou Zhonghe, Institute of Vertebrate Paleontology and Paleoanthropology, China; p.177 © De Agostini/NHMPL; p.181 © Photograph by Herb Meyer, provided courtesy of Florissant Fossil Beds National Monument; p.189 (l) *Annals of Botany*, 50:569-583, Friis & Skarby, © Oxford University Press, (r) *Nature*, 291:485-486, Friis & Skarby, 1981, © Macmillan Publishers Ltd; p.192 *Annals of the Missouri Botanical Garden*, 72: 4, Crane, 1985; p.193 (l) © K. Simons, D. Dilcher, G. Sun & T. Lott; p.178 (r) © D. Dilcher, G. Sun, Q. Ji & T. Lott; p.197 *Nature*, 374:27-33, Crane, Friis & Pedersen, 1995, © Macmillan Publishers Ltd; p.200 Amended from *Nature*, 410:357-360, Kenrick, 1999, © Macmillan Publishers Ltd; p.201 *Nature*, 402:358-359, Friis, Pedersen & Crane, 2001, © Macmillan Publishers Ltd.

NHM, Natural History Museum, London; NHMPL, Natural History Museum Picture Library